WISDOM OF THE
NATURAL
WORLD

About the Author

"I am here to inspire, encourage, and empower you to be your authentic self."

Joy "Granddaughter Crow" Gray has received a BS in business management as well as a BS in business administration, an MBA, and a doctorate in leadership. She has several years of experience in corporate America working for an international company and additional time working for the government, and has worked as a college professor. She is here to share and serve under the name of Granddaughter Crow.

Internationally recognized as a Medicine Woman, Granddaughter Crow was born an empath and medium. She comes from a long lineage of spiritual leaders and esoteric wisdom. Raised by spiritual leaders, as a child she was fashioned and trained to serve the people through ministry. She is a member of the Navajo Nation (50 percent) and also has Dutch heritage (50 percent). Granddaughter Crow provides a sense of integration through life experience.

Granddaughter Crow was inducted into the Delta Mu Delta International Honors Society in 2012, was voted Woman of the Year 2015 by the National Association of Professional Women (NAPW), and was featured in *Native Max Magazine*'s June/July 2016 issue.

In 2014, Granddaughter Crow founded the Eagle Heart Foundation, a 501(c)(3) nonprofit organization dedicated to charitable giving and educational enhancement of the Native American population for the purpose of honoring the ancestors and responding to their heartfelt prayers.

Granddaughter Crow ®

WISDOM OF THE
NATURAL
WORLD

Spiritual and Practical Teachings from
Plants, Animals
& Mother Earth

GRANDDAUGHTER CROW

Llewellyn Publications
Woodbury, Minnesota

FIRST EDITION
First Printing, 2021

Book design by Samantha Peterson
Cover design by Shannon McKuhen
Granddaughter Crow Logo on page iv provided by the author
Interior art by Llewellyn Art Department
Vetruvian Man on page 27 by Eugene Smith

Llewellyn Publications is a registered trademark of Llewellyn Worldwide Ltd.

Library of Congress Cataloging-in-Publication Data
Names: Gray, Joy, author.
Title: Wisdom of the natural world : spiritual and practical teachings from
    plants, animals & Mother Earth / Granddaughter Crow.
Description: First edition. | Woodbury, MN : Llewellyn Worldwide, Ltd,
    2021. | Includes bibliographical references. | Summary: "Featuring
    profound insights from the plant and animal kingdoms and beyond, this
    empowering guide uses natural wisdom to help you find balance in life"—
    Provided by publisher.
Identifiers: LCCN 2020050978 (print) | LCCN 2020050979 (ebook) | ISBN
    9780738766300 | ISBN 9780738766553 (ebook)
Subjects: LCSH: Nature—Religious aspects.
Classification: LCC BL65.N35 G46 2021 (print) | LCC BL65.N35 (ebook) |
    DDC 202/.12—dc23
LC record available at https://lccn.loc.gov/2020050978
LC ebook record available at https://lccn.loc.gov/2020050979

Llewellyn Worldwide Ltd. does not participate in, endorse, or have any authority or responsibility concerning private business transactions between our authors and the public.
    All mail addressed to the author is forwarded but the publisher cannot, unless specifically instructed by the author, give out an address or phone number.
    Any internet references contained in this work are current at publication time, but the publisher cannot guarantee that a specific location will continue to be maintained. Please refer to the publisher's website for links to authors' websites and other sources.

Llewellyn Publications
A Division of Llewellyn Worldwide Ltd.
2143 Wooddale Drive
Woodbury, MN 55125-2989
www.llewellyn.com

Printed in the United States of America

Other Books by Granddaughter Crow

The Journey of the Soul

This book is dedicated to the past, present, and future. I dedicate this book to my grandfather, a man whom I have never met in the flesh, but I know him through the blood that runs through my veins. Hence, I am Granddaughter Crow. I dedicate this book to my husband, Jeffrey Gray. Without him, I would not be this far along on my journey. I dedicate this book to my son, Michael Major. Without him, I would not be who I am. Do we raise our children, or do they raise us as parents? I dedicate this book to my grandchildren, for they hold our future. Blessings to all.

Contents

List of Exercises • *xiii*

The Navajo Beauty Way Prayer • *xv*

Foreword • *xvii*

Introduction • *1*

One: Connecting and Learning through Nature • 9

Two: The Animal Kingdom • 35

Three: The Plant Kingdom • 69

Four: Landscapes • 91

Five: The Seasons and Weather Cycles • 107

Six: The Medicine Wheel • 129

Seven: The Shadow Self • 163

Eight: Empowerment • 183

Conclusion • *195*

Bibliography • *199*

Exercises

Exercise 1: Reacquaint with Nature • 12

Exercise 2: Mindfulness • 14

Exercise 3: Breathing • 23

Exercise 4: Body Is a Pendulum • 29

Exercise 5: Animal Totem • 43

Exercise 6: Diagnose the Four Bodies of Existence • 57

Exercise 7: Plant Totem • 80

Exercise 8: Relationship • 113

Exercise 9: Career • 117

Exercise 10: Be a Tree • 124

Exercise 11: Listening Circle • 147

Exercise 12: Finances • 151

Exercise 13: Team Building • 185

Exercise 14: Medicine Wheel • 189

The Navajo Beauty Way Prayer

In beauty I walk
With beauty before me I walk
With beauty behind me I walk
With beauty above me I walk
With beauty around me I walk
It has become beauty again
It has become beauty again
It has become beauty again
It has become beauty again

Hózhóogo naasháa doo
Shitsijí' hózhóogo naasháa doo
Shikéédéé hózhóogo naasháa doo
Shideigi hózhóogo naasháa doo
T'áá altso shinaagóó hózhóogo naasháa doo
Hózhó náhásdlíí'
Hózhó náhásdlíí'
Hózhó náhásdlíí'
Hózhó náhásdlíí'

Foreword

Breathe in. Now breathe out. You have just experienced a complete cycle of life. You have experienced, in that simple moment, a microcosm of the entire universe.

"Come take a stroll with me," invites Granddaughter Crow in the pages of this beautiful book, one that will allow you to experience yourself, perhaps for the first time, as an integral and important part of the natural world. As a part of the whole that is needed. Necessary—required—in order for the entire Universe to function. In order for the entire Universe to exist. You, yes, YOU, you are that important. And in the following pages, you'll see, feel, hear, and know that you are both unique and also similar to many of the other parts of the Universe, the great "medicine wheel" of creation.

Your decision to be here at this moment in time is a reflection of the movement of the cosmos into something beautiful, reverent, sacred, and true: balance. That is what everything under the sun exists to achieve: Harmony. Peace. Balance.

By applying the concepts of the natural world to your everyday life, Granddaughter Crow both illuminates the natural world and all its wonders into the wisdom of your mental body and associated language and grounds that knowledge into the wisdom of your soul.

The goal? To walk in balance in all areas of your life: career and work; relationships, both loving romantic relationships and all relationships with others, including the natural world. Wondering how to coexist at work with others who seem so different to you? Just apply the lessons of the trees—who stand tall—or perhaps you want to be more like a bush, which lies low to the ground and blends in. Wondering how to find balance in your romantic relationship? Perhaps you can call on the energies of the animal kingdom and find your inner wolf, the protector who sees what's ahead on the ground. Or perhaps you can channel your inner crow or raven, the one who sees the big picture and can have visionary ideas and yes, even magic.

Balance. For years, I've referred to this word as "the Divine B" word. It's something that everything in existence seeks. Homeostasis is another word for what we *all* seek. To ebb or flow, to peak or valley, to rise or fall, to move left or right; it's all part of the process of "listening" to the natural rhythms that are inherent in the greater whole. Then decide if it's in your own or the collective best interest to flow with the larger rhythm or, perhaps, find your own rhythm that goes against the larger flow, like a salmon does. No choice is worse than the other. Your own walk, your own path, is what Granddaughter Crow is inviting you to find.

So in this book, in the following pages, play around a bit with the beauty of life. Embrace that you might, today, in this moment, want to be a mountain, while tomorrow, it might be in your best interest to work with the energy of the lake or ocean.

Animals, elements, plants, seasons, environment, and planets ... they are all forces that are larger than us, yet they are also, paradoxically, part of us. Connecting to these parts of us is one of the goals of living a life that is balanced. Whole. Integrated. Complete. Just like the circle.

Set aside any notions of right or wrong. Let Granddaughter Crow guide you into the great mystery. Her words will illuminate your soul and light your Divine spark. You'll understand, for perhaps the first time, that you are here on this earth for a reason, and because you exist, you are achieving your life mission and purpose simply by breathing.

So whatever reason has brought you to the pages of this book, keep allowing that energy of inquiry to move you into the next phase of your growth. Your awakening is about to be deepened, and your intentions amplified, by realizing that you are important to the cosmos, just as the cosmos is important to you.

So, sink in, let go, and allow ...

Be blessed on your journey.

Aho. *Mitakue Oyasin.* (We are all related.) We are all One.

—Michael R. Smith, PhD
empathconnection.com

Introduction

The natural world embodies wisdom and insight for the human race. No matter what you are facing within your experience, the natural world can reveal many alternative perspectives that you may not have initially considered. From animals and plants to landscapes and seasons, the natural world is a great teacher. It can guide us and support us with relationships and romance, business affairs and finance, and health and well-being.

Life is all about relationships. It's about how we interact and connect with the world around us—our relationships with others; our relationship to finances and business affairs; our relationship with our physical bodies and our health. Additionally, our relationship with the natural world. The natural world was here before us. It is continuously adapting and rebalancing to sustain life force. Within the natural world, there are countless numbers of species and organisms which work together to create Earth's biosphere. The natural world is ancient and wise; hence, I recognize it as our eldest wisdom keeper. It can teach us many things if we pay attention, if we are mindful.

The natural world does not forget that it is the natural world—humans forget. We forget that we are a part of the natural world. We like to say that we are going into nature for a retreat, but the truth is that we *are* nature. We have separated ourselves from who and what we are.

We have forgotten many things about how to balance, to belong, to become. We can talk so intelligently about all of our confusion, but don't get lost in the confusion. May we remember that we are a part of the natural world, and may we remember how to apply the wisdom of the natural world to our lives in order to be the best version of ourselves. The human population has been on Mother Earth for thousands and thousands of years. That sounds like a long time; however, it is just long enough to forget who and what we are. We are nature, and we are a part of the natural world. All the reminders of these ancient lessons are still here. They are provided to us by our greatest and eldest teacher, the natural world.

If I were to ask a tree, "What gives you the right to be here? What gives you permission to grow so tall? What gave you permission to be authentic?" The tree wouldn't answer my questions. Yet, I may struggle with my sense of belonging, limiting myself, and being afraid to be authentic. The human race is the only organism that I have found that will struggle with such ludicrous concepts: the concept of not belonging, or not being who and what we authentically are as individuals. Why do we do this? Is it natural? Or is this an idea that we created? I do not believe that these concepts are natural. Moreover, I believe that these concepts were introduced to us ages ago by other humans in order to have power and control over others, yet they are so ingrained within our psyche that we believe them to be true—we may even believe that they are natural. I am on a mission to investigate the natural world and to extract the wisdom that it holds. Please join me.

Background on Your Tour Guide

We are about to embrace this journey together, so I'd like to give you a little insight into who I am. *Ya'at'eeh* ("hello" in Navajo). I am Granddaughter Crow (also known as Dr. Joy Gray). The traditional way to introduce myself in Navajo is to tell you what clan I am born "to" (mother's clan) and what clan I am born "for" (father's clan). I am born to the Biligaana clan and born for the Tachii'nii clan. In short, another Navajo would recognize that my mother is Caucasian and my father is full-blood Navajo. I am a bridge between two cultures; I have found that respecting each culture and its traditions is very important. Hence, when I am referencing something from my Navajo culture, I will let you know. Moreover, when speaking about the natural world and how we can relate to the natural world, regardless of background, my hope is that we all remember that we come from Mother Earth—Mother Earth is exactly that, our mother.

Additionally, I speak about relationships, business, and health within these pages. I have informally studied relationships and health because I am very drawn to each of these topics. Yes, I am the person at the bookstore in the self-help section—I'm not much of a fiction reader. I do have two undergraduate degrees in business, a master of business administration, and a doctorate in leadership and organizational development, so I did learn a little bit about relationships in my studies. In 2008 I opened Major Consulting LLC. Currently, I am internationally recognized as a Medicine Woman and come from a long lineage of spiritual leaders and esoteric wisdom. Raised by spiritual leaders, I was fashioned and trained to serve the people through ministry.

My hope is that this journey together will provide you with other ways to approach your life, other ways to connect with the natural world, and other ways of thinking and being. I would like to inspire, encourage, and empower you to be your authentic self. I wrote this book with the hope that it would feel like I am conversing with you, so as you read, please feel free to set the book down from time to time and journal your thoughts on the topic. I have also provided you with a few exercises throughout the book that can lead to further self-knowledge. Above all else, I hope that you find your authenticity and become more of your empowered self. The world wouldn't be the same without you.

Let's Begin Our Journey

Have you ever heard about the Sapir-Whorf hypothesis or linguist determinism? Each one of these concepts suggests that the language that we speak has a direct impact on the way that we think. This hypothesis states that our language shapes our reality. Moreover, the pattern of thought is directly influenced by the language we speak. The language that we speak may have limitations; hence, our thoughts may have limitations. The concept that linguistic structure determines cognitive structure is mind-altering. The language that we speak will limit or determine our thought process and our worldview in general. The correlations between our thoughts and the language that we speak is fascinating. Although there are those who will claim that this is not true in all situations, I believe that the language that we speak has an impact on the way that we think and vice versa. For example, in the Alaskan Yupik language, there are approximately fifteen different words to describe snow. The people think more intelligently about the snow because their language holds more sophisticated and subtle words distinguishing the different types of snow.[1] Hence, their language allows them to understand snow more than someone who may live within the desert.

I will give you a direct example of this and how it can apply to us communicating with the natural world. This may assist you to step outside the box of the language that we speak and begin to understand the intelligence of nature. Imagine that you are standing before a tree and someone asks you to get to know this tree. Although there are many ways to get to know a tree, here is an example of two very different ways of experiencing and knowing a tree. Biologically, I am 50 percent Navajo and 50 percent Dutch, so I think in both cultures and in both the Navajo and English languages. The language of any culture is a direct reflection of the cognitive worldview of said culture. The English language speaks in terms of labels or naming things, segregating and separating things in order to break them down into smaller parts in order to understand each part and the whole. Hence, in order to get to know the tree as an English speaker, one would have to segregate and separate the parts and then name the parts in order to know the tree. For example, the tree has roots, a trunk, branches, and leaves. It has a genus with a scientific name; in this case, let's say we're looking at an oak tree.

However, there is another way of getting to know the tree. The Navajo language describes things and sees things as a part of the whole. One can only know a tree when one experiences a connection to the tree. In order to get to know the tree, one would stand before the tree and notice the complete organism. Next, they would notice that the leaves of the tree are moving in one gentle

---

1. Woodbury, *Counting Eskimo Words for Snow.*

direction. Then, one would notice that their own hair is moving in the same direction. At this point, they would connect with the tree and recognize that there is something, a force, that is moving them and the tree in the same way. This is how they know the tree. I am not suggesting that you think in one way or another, as there are many different ways to experience the tree. Maybe you have a different type of relationship to a tree. Maybe it was a landmark for you, or you have great memories of climbing the tree as a child. I am inviting you to consider all ways and to find the balance within. Do not forget your own totality—your wholeness.

The natural world can be cold, harsh, and dangerous at times. This allowed me to understand that while life can be difficult, that is simply the way it is. It is hard; indeed it is. Yet the sun continues to come up. The spring will follow the winter—the warmth, fluidity, and peace will return. This is the cycle that nature reveals to us.

I started beholding the natural world and my life changed. When I realized that I am a part of the natural world, I gained a sense of belonging, belonging to something that is so much greater than myself. When I began to observe the natural world, I began to recognize that it was observing me as well. The birds that visit my backyard know that I live here. I put food out for them and created a birdbath for them. Now, I can hear them singing every morning. I have a sense that the birds are not only communicating with each other, but they are communicating with me, too. They do not judge me for the clothes that I am wearing or what my hair looks like. They simply sense me. I feel encouraged to be my authentic self.

Not only can the natural world provide us with a sense of belonging and an encouragement to be our authentic self, but the natural world also holds many wise insights for us on how to live, love, and be the best version of self. I have found this to be true, and now I want to share these concepts with you.

In this book, we will examine the natural concepts within the animal kingdom, the plant kingdom, landscapes, seasons, and weather cycles. Once we begin to discover these concepts, we will look at how to apply the wise insights from each and every one of them into our day-to-day lives. First things first: How do we connect and communicate with the natural world if it doesn't speak our language?

ONE
Connecting and Learning through Nature

How do we learn through nature? It is simply a different thought process when we are approaching the natural world as a teacher. Nature has likely been our teacher throughout history. It is possible that wolves taught humans how to hunt. Maybe birds taught humans how to sing. Maybe trees taught humans how to stand tall. Of course, I am merely speculating, as there is not written history of what our ancestors experienced. However, there are petroglyphs on the walls of caves which hold pictures of humankind, the natural world, and human interaction with the natural world and our relationship with it. You may experience a sense of familiarity as we move through this book.

First, we will look at how we can dialogue with nature in order to extract various concepts that can then be applied to our lives.

Another step is to become more mindful of what we are experiencing as we move throughout our lives on a day-to-day basis. The natural world holds a variety of relations as it works to survive, thrive, and continuously rebalance itself. We can extract these lessons and apply them to our personal relationships and romance, to business and finance, and to our health and well-being. Additionally, the natural world is a holistic organism with millions of moving parts, yet it has a way of balancing these parts. We can break down these concepts as we look at the medicine wheel. Finally, the natural world can assist us with the concept of the shadow self. When we approach the topic of the shadow self, it can be frightening; however, the natural world can walk us through the process. Let's begin!

Dialogue with Nature

Communication is key in all relationships. It is how we interact—it's how we understand and express. So, if it is so vital, how do we communicate with the natural world? It may be easier than you think; you may already be doing it without realizing it. Let's begin by opening up our dialogue with nature.

The etymology of the word *dialogue* comes from the Greek word *dialogos*, *dia* meaning "through" and *logos* meaning "reason." Dialogue is a type of communication that promotes wholeness rather than division. Dialogue occurs when we decide how to reason or think together—and when this occurs, a common mind will arise.[2] It creates shared meaning—a stream of meaning flowing between us, through us, and among us. It connects us to each other and to nature.

---

2. Bohm and Weinberg, *On Dialogue*, xviii.

Within communication, there is both verbal and nonverbal communication. Did you know that only 7 percent of communication is actually achieved via words or text? This means 93 percent of communication comes from cues rather than words. Here is the actual breakdown:

1. Seven percent of communication is a result of verbal words.

2. Thirty-eight percent of communication is a result of vocal tones, pitch, and rhythm.

3. Fifty-five percent of communication is a result of body language, including facial expressions.[3]

I imagine this is why people created emojis—in order to make up for the remaining ninety-three percent of communication cues that are missing when we text or type. The natural world isn't necessarily speaking to us in dialogue, but it is still speaking with us.

If you think about it, we already work with the symbols of the natural world within analogies that we use. For example, we may refer to people as "a night owl" or "cool as a cucumber." We refer to situations with comments like "the perfect storm," "it's going to be clear skies from here on out," or "this is a breeze." The natural world provides us with helpful symbols to assist us in communicating with others.

The natural world is constantly communicating … if we listen. So, how does one listen to nature? Begin by observing the various behaviors found in the natural world—be within the moment. Be mindful. Observe nature constantly adjusting and reestablishing a balance within itself. We may need to translate it into English in

3. Koneya and Barbour, *Louder Than Words*, 4.

order to understand it more fully, but that simply takes practice. For example, the animal kingdom may share insights with us that we can see by noticing the way animals survive, hunt, mate, sleep, and move. The plant kingdom may share insights with us via the way plants grow, where they grow, and how they survive in the world. Landscapes can show us the environments that are present within any culture or subculture (including friends and family). Seasons and weather cycles can show us the overarching atmosphere of any given situation and that everything continuously ebbs and flows. Nature provides us with wise insights for any circumstance.

The natural world holds symbology. For example, two areas rich with symbology are the inner world and the outer world. The inner world could be represented by winter, by night, or by caverns. When we experience these things, we tend to go within and withdraw. The outer world could be represented by summer, by day, or by open meadows. When we experience these things, we tend to expand outward. Keep this in mind as you observe the world around you.

✦✦✦ EXERCISE 1 ✦✦✦
Reacquaint with Nature

To do this exercise, pick a place outside—any natural place works—that you will be able to access multiple times throughout the day. Stand or sit in this place four times during the day: in the morning, at noon, in the evening, and at night. Begin to become aware of any differences that you may notice depending on what time of day it is. The sun and moon will draw out many differences. In the morning, the sun will cast a shadow toward the west; the sun in the evening will do the opposite. Sense these differences with your body, feel them with your heart, and begin to place adjectives around what you are sensing. The adjectives are your way of placing words around what it is communicating with you. Also, do not be afraid of misinterpreting it. Although it may say one thing to me, it may say something different to you. This is the beauty and complexity of our teacher, revealing meaning and messages to each of us. If it helps, give that place a name and connect with it all the more.

Once we observe natural behaviors, it is a good practice to reflect on the experience through writing. When we take time to reflect, deeper meanings will come to the surface. For example, if I see a butterfly and want to understand what the butterfly is talking about, I can sit back and watch what it is doing. Next, I might write about what I observed like this: "The beautiful butterfly was dancing on the tips of the flowers. As she danced, it was as though she was showing off how light and beautiful she can be in the world." Hence, the butterfly was reminding me to move through my day with a lightness of heart and spirit. Here is another example: When I get confused, I go to a maple tree and tell it all my thoughts and I feel better. It is amazing what the maple tree will show me. At times, it shows me to stand tall and to not allow the winds within my mind to break me. It tells me to allow the winds within my thoughts to blow through my mind because soon they will settle.

Mindfulness

Being mindful is powerful—mindfulness is the ability to be in the moment and experience all that the moment holds. Over the past couple of decades, there has been an increased focus on mindfulness and its benefits. Mindfulness can reduce stress, increase focus and concentration, and positively impact overall health on physical, emotional, mental, and spiritual levels.

Mindfulness can begin with a certain type of meditation called *satipatthana* mindfulness meditation. *Satipatthana* means to keep your attention inside. There are many forms of meditation. Some ask you to empty your mind; this is not that kind of meditation. Mindfulness meditation simply asks an individual to pay attention to what is going on within themselves as they move throughout the day. The concept is to be present within each moment and to train the brain to gently come back from its wondering. There are so many things within our society that will distract us. At times we are multitasking but getting nothing done; driving fast, but getting nowhere. I once heard that the human mind will wander off over forty percent of the time if untrained to focus. It is not necessarily a bad thing for the mind to wander; however, the mind would become much stronger if it could behold each and every moment with consciousness—if it could be present and mindful.

✦✦✦ EXERCISE 2 ✦✦✦
Mindfulness

Bring your full attention to your inhales and exhales: the expansion on the inhale, the release on the exhale. Simply notice that you are breathing in. Simply notice that you are breathing out. Now, withdraw your attention from the external world and relax. Do a body scan and release any and all tension. Become aware of yourself and breathe.

Start each day with this meditation and begin to apply this mindfulness in your life as you move throughout the day. You will become more and more present and connected.

They teach mindfulness in some schools now. Some healthcare fields are using it to help their patients with all types of physical, emotional, and mental imbalances. Also, I've learned that there is a program within some prisons that teaches inmates how to practice mindfulness. The work begins with a breath and paying attention to each moment.

There is a monk who was born in Nepal by the name of Yongey Mingyur Rinpoche. The story goes that when he was young, he suffered from panic attacks, so his father taught him how to meditate. The first thing his father asked him to do was to focus on his breath as he inhaled and exhaled. Whenever the mind wandered off, his father taught him to gently bring it back to the breath. That was the beginning of Rinpoche's mindfulness journey; now he is known as a mindfulness meditation prodigy. When he was forty-one years old, the scientific community became interested in his brain and the effects mindfulness has on the human brain. Although he was forty-one, he had the brain of a thirty-three year old: a physical manifestation of the benefits of mindfulness.[4]

Emotionally and mentally, mindfulness gives us permission to become aware of how we are feeling and what we are thinking within a moment. The idea is that we learn to approach our inner world with awareness and compassion, releasing any judgments. This can lead us to a deeper connection with our emotions

---

4. Rinpoche and Swanson, *Joy of Living*, 4.

and thoughts. Rinpoche still experienced panic, but he eventually befriended it. To him, panic is simply a rush of adrenaline that he can tap into to get him moving throughout his day. He was no longer fearfully anticipating a panic attack, which prolongs the experience.

Fear of that which may come is a lot of wasted energy. When I was a teenager, I had a test in school that I didn't prepare for. For half of the day, I was worried about this test. Then a thought came to me: "Why am I spending my whole day worrying about something that will be over in less than an hour?" I decided to let go and let it be. Today, I can't remember the test or how I performed, but I can remember that wisdom. I was wasting hours sitting in fear and worry. I think that was my first experience with mindfulness.

The spiritual impact of mindfulness is an individual journey and discovery; however, I have met many mindful individuals and they all seem more peaceful. Mindful people notice the beauty of the world that we live in. They tend to be more understanding and compassionate. Let's become aware of what we are focusing on. I once heard a statement that went something like "What you practice grows stronger." I don't want to become a stressed out, bitter old woman—I am becoming a wise, youthful woman. This spiritual journey is very important to me.

As I continue to be present within my life and allow the natural world to communicate with me in a mindful way, I am being enlightened.

The next three sections will introduce how to directly apply the wisdom of the natural world to our relationships and romance, careers and finance, and health and well-being. These sections are simply an introduction to the thought process of learning through nature and being mindful of the natural world's dialogue, as it is communicating with us. Additionally, within many of the chapters of this book, deeper applications will be provided. I hope you are enjoying this adventure into the natural world as our eldest teacher.

Relationships & Romance

There are so many different types of relationships. There are family relationships, friends and acquaintances, and our relationships with colleagues, just to name a few. Of course, there are also romantic relationships; the natural world can assist us with understanding this type of dynamic as well. There is a section on relationships and romance within most chapters of this book. In each of these sections, you can apply the wisdom that the natural world provides to any and all of these types of relationships.

In general, I like to see relationships as a dance between the self and the other(s). At times we will dance with the other(s). We begin to establish the pace of the relationship with the other(s), the positions (how close or how much space), and the rhythm and reason of the relationship. Additionally, we establish the give and the take, the balance, and if one is going to lead. We establish this dance at the beginning of the relationship. However, at times one person or the other will decide that they would like to dance in a different way. This can cause problems if one partner is unaware of this change, and the two can begin to step on each other's toes if they are not careful.

For example, maybe two individuals meet and establish their relationship flows in a type of line dance. This works great until one individual decides that they also would like to do the tango. These are two very different styles. If this is not communicated, then they will begin to step on each other's toes, and it could become the image of a fight. Line dancing and the tango are both wonderful dances; however, we simply need to understand which dance we are doing in each relationship. If you'd like to change the pace or do another type of dance, discuss this with your partner. Change is good, but learn how to move together in harmony.

There are also times when one may decide to get off the dance floor and catch their breath. This works too. When a person leaves a relationship and is a little discombobulated or confused, I recommend that they take up some dancing lessons. In the dancing lesson, they learn how to move in and out and how to give and receive. The student learns how they like to dance and it re-centers their understanding of what they need within a relationship. It may sound funny, but I have seen it work. Give it a try if you find yourself in a similar situation and want to understand relationships more.

The natural world moves in a rhythm and a pattern. There are many patterns and movements in nature. Some organisms may flow together; others may represent the predator and prey; still others may stay away from one another. Be that as it may, the natural world can show us how to be with others.

Business & Finance

We all have our own relationship with business and finance. How do we approach our career and/or business? What is our relationship with our finances? The natural world can assist us with this dynamic, as it holds many lessons within it.

For example, I may approach my career and/or my finances as a type of animal. I may approach it as a lion or as a hawk. A lion approaches things with power and poise; it hunts quietly and pounces with ferocity. A hawk may approach things from a bird's-eye view and swoop in for the taking. If I approached my career and/or finances as an ant, I would be a team player looking for other team players, as ants work in colonies. Think about how the animal you have chosen approaches things and moves within the world, then consider using that approach in regard to your career and/or finances. Of course, you can change your position if you wish.

The plant kingdom can reveal lessons to us here as well. Maybe a person approaches their career like a vine: they find other strong people and begin to climb them for support in order to reach their goals. Vines are adaptable and free-forming. This may sound a little odd, but it is a lesson that nature provides to us. Maybe someone approaches their finances like a tree; it takes time to grow a tree, but they are self-made and strong individuals.

There are different landscapes and/or environments within each industry and within the financial markets. At times it is like a jungle and we need to be tigers. Other times it may be like the desert and we need to conserve, be patient, and be resourceful. If we understand what landscape we are in, we are able to adapt to that landscape as plants and animals adapt to the environment.

There are business cycles and/or seasons. There is a season to start something new, to grow something that was planted, and to harvest. There is also a season to simply hold and sustain. Have you ever heard the saying "make hay while the sun is shining"? This is an example of our understanding of these seasons. There are also weather patterns within each of these seasons. At times, it may be sunny, rainy, or stormy. A storm may destroy our career or finances. The storm will eventually pass, but make sure that you plan ahead for that rainy day. Rain will fall in everyone's lifetime— it is not a punishment; it is the way of the natural world. If you plan for each season and weather pattern, you will be fine. Nature teaches us how to survive within it.

Health & Well-Being

There is a school of thought that we have four bodies of existence: the physical body, the emotional body, the mental body, and the spiritual body. These four bodies combined make up an individual. Although there may be more bodies of existence, we will work with this model of four bodies as a starting point.

The physical body is tangible and solid, like the earth. It holds a physical age, a certain physical maturity. The physical body is a part of nature (earth) just like the trees—it is strong, balanced, and in a continuous state of self-healing and rebalancing. Our physical body needs nourishment, rest, and exercise to remain healthy and fit. The nourishment that we feed our physical body is food. In order to rest the physical body, we can relax or sleep. The exercise that we do to keep it fit and strong requires physical exertion.

While our physical bodies correspond to the strength of the earth, our emotional bodies are fluid and flow like water. The physical body holds an emotional age; however, the emotional age is not necessarily in direct correlation to the physical age. Emotionally, I can feel four years old in one moment and forty years old in another, depending on what I am encountering. Have you ever encountered an individual who is fifty years old physically, yet emotionally responds as a five-year-old in certain situations? Moreover, have you ever encountered a ten-year-old who holds the maturity of an elder? Emotions move like water—they can be refreshing as they ebb and flow. They can come in waves, moving through you and at times overtaking you. They can be stagnant, lacking movement and even sinking into a depressed state. The emotional body needs nourishment, rest, and exercise to remain healthy and fit. The best nourishment we can give our emotional body is positive emotion such as understanding, love, grace, peace, and joy, to name a few. The emotional body needs rest (downtime) in order to maintain health. Emotional rest can be found in acts of peacefulness and calmness. There are many ways that we can enter an emotional state of peacefulness and calmness. What works best for you? Exercising our emotional body can be accomplished with an open heart and connecting with the world around us.

Our physical bodies correspond to the earth. Our emotional bodies flow like water. Our mental bodies behave much like the wind—they move like the air. Thoughts flow in and out; at times they can be as random as a breeze. They can spin like the spiral of a funnel cloud, up and out, or spiral into themselves like the eye of a hurricane. They can be calm or calming.

According to Alfred Binet, who published the first intelligence test in 1911, our mental body has an age.[5] Binet's test was adopted a few years later by Lewis Terman, a psychologist at Stanford University, and resulted in the common IQ test that we know today.[6] The basic concept measured mental age, whereas the revised system measures the intelligence quotient within a percentile system. The percentile system uses one hundred points as the average score; hence, approximately 50 percent of the population will score one hundred points on the test. Approximately 95 percent of the population will score between seventy and 130 points, leaving a very small percentage to score above or below this range. Mental age, like the ebbs and flows of the air, can change depending on an individual and the situation. When an individual is tired, hungry, stressed, or simply not feeling well, it will impact their mental age. Therefore, mental age can move backward and forward in its maturity. The mental body needs nourishment, rest, and exercise to remain healthy and fit—food for thought. Consider an idea that

5. Miller, *The Test*, 55–58.

6. Lemann, *The IQ Meritocracy*, 115–16.

you haven't had before; this not only feeds the mind, but it exercises it as well. An individual does not need to adopt every thought that travels through their mind; some thoughts simply need to be recognized and released. It takes a strong mind to entertain a thought that it does not adopt. The ability to hold a thought and focus on that thought takes a healthy mind.

It is worth mentioning that mental intelligence is not the only type of intelligence we have. In 1983, Howard Gardner introduced the theory of multiple intelligence. This theory suggests that traditional psychometric views of intelligence are too limited. Different types of intelligence can be housed in our mental body, physical body, emotional body, and spiritual body. Gardner outlines his theory, suggesting that there are nine different types of intellect to date:

- Naturalist intelligence (nature smart)
- Musical intelligence (musical smart)
- Logical-mathematical intelligence (number/reasoning smart)
- Interpersonal intelligence (people smart)
- Bodily-kinesthetic intelligence (body smart)
- Linguistic intelligence (word smart)
- Intrapersonal intelligence (self smart)
- Spatial intelligence (picture smart)
- Existential intelligence (philosophy and spiritual smart; the intelligence of big questions such as "What is the meaning of life?")[7]

---

7. Gardner, *Frames of Mind*, 282.

Flowing from this list, existential intelligence can touch on and lead us beyond philosophy and toward spirituality. The spiritual body is inspirational—it is like fire. It can purify and keep us energized and inspired. The age of a spiritual body can fluctuate and expand past the physical, emotional, and mental bodies, hence the saying, "That person is an old soul." I have found that when an individual begins their personal spiritual path, they may do so for one of two very different reasons: one reason is to grow and develop; the other reason is to escape from reality. Like a baby, the spirit is awakened. It is nurtured and watched over by another. However, at the spiritual age of approximately two years old, the caregivers will begin to show the young spirit how to take care of themselves. As the spirit develops more and more, the individual has more and more responsibility to attend to itself and to the world. If an individual is on the spiritual path in order to escape from reality, the individual usually abandons said path once they are required to assume spiritual responsibility. The nourishment for the spiritual body comes in many forms; there are many spiritual paths. However, most spiritual paths have one thing in common: the spirit must be nourished.

✛✛✛ **EXERCISE 3** ✛✛✛
Breathing

One way to reset all four bodies (mental, physical, emotional, spiritual) at the same time is by engaging in the following activity: breathing! The threefold breath is an exercise that simultaneously benefits our physical, emotional, mental, and spiritual bodies. The first fold is the inhale through the nose. The second fold is to hold the breath within the physical body. The third fold is to exhale and release, again through the nose. Inhaling and exhaling through the nose (rather than the mouth) will activate the parasympathetic nervous system for quick relaxation.

Each of these three folds is given a certain count and cadence that works best for the individual. For example, inhale for four counts, hold for four counts, and exhale for six counts. I encourage every individual to find the count and cadence that works best for them. If you do this exercise for three minutes in the morning and three minutes in the evening, it begins to reset the physical nervous system and relaxes emotional and mental bodies. It also opens up the spiritual body.

Working with this type of breathing takes us from the beta state into an alpha state. An alpha state is a more relaxed state which impacts all four bodies. Some of the many benefits of increasing alpha state include deep relaxation of the emotional and mental bodies, increased levels of creativity, more focus and improved problem-solving skills, increased ability to learn something new, and increased serotonin levels.[8] Serotonin is a chemical that directly impacts our mood, contributing to a sense of well-being and happiness.

Here is the basic list of states of consciousness that each of us may enter: beta, alpha, theta, and delta. As the scientific community continues to research states of consciousness, they may find more than these basic four (such as gamma state).

---

8. McCullough, "Alpha State."

Beta state is when an individual is fully awake and completely active. In this state, the brain waves operate at a level called beta where brainwaves mainly oscillate between fourteen to forty cycles per second.

Alpha state is when an individual's mind is relaxed and the person enters a more focused, expanded state of awareness. Alpha brain wave patterns oscillate between nine and thirteen cycles per second.

Theta state is when an individual relaxes even more and the mind enters a region that correlates with brain wave patterns of five to eight cycles per second. This is the theta zone of the mind. One can experience profound creativity, characterized by feelings of inspiration and spirituality.

Delta state is the level of the mysterious universal mind. It is the level at which the differentiated self (ego) expands to become undifferentiated and operates outside of the confines of linear time/space. In delta state, the brain waves are between one and a half and four cycles per second.[9] This is also recognized as deep sleep.

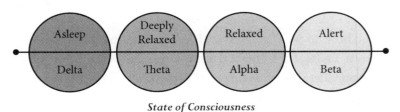

State of Consciousness

Considering that we have four bodies of existence, we can easily recognize that each of these bodies has a maturity level, a need for

---

9. Herrmann, "What Is the Function of the Various Brainwaves?"

nourishment, a need for rest, and a need for exercise. However, the physical body is the only one of these four that is subjected and confined to space and linear time (for the most part). The other three bodies can move in and out of space and time with ease. For example, if you were to recall a wonderful memory and sit with it for a moment, you may have a physical, mental, emotional, and/or spiritual reaction as though the wonderful moment is happening in the moment. Additionally, if you were to visualize a wonderful future and what that would be like, you may have a physical, mental, emotional, and/or spiritual sensation as though this is happening in the moment. Taking time to feed, rest, exercise, and listen to each of these four bodies assists us in experiencing a more balanced and harmonious existence.

So how do these bodies work together? Moreover, what happens when they are not in alignment with each other? Have you ever physically been in one place, yet your emotions are somewhere else, your mind is in yet another place, and your spirit is just silent because you're in too many places at one time? I have. I feel lost at these times—like I am not in the right place. Perhaps this is because I am in too many places at one time, which can toss anyone out of balance and equilibrium.

So how do we change this? How do we align our four bodies? There is a school of thought that the *Vitruvian Man* by Leonardo da Vinci provides us with a portrait of balance, proportion, alignment, and equilibrium. In this image, one can theoretically see the four bodies working together. Although I do not know the depths of all that da Vinci portrayed in this masterpiece, and although I cannot confirm that he was depicting these four bodies, I can say that this model directly aligns with this school of thought.

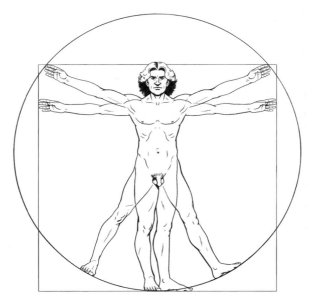

Example of the **Vitruvian Man**

The physical body is depicted by the body standing straight with its legs together and its arms directly outstretched. The emotional body is depicted by the body that appears to be in motion, with the legs spread and the arms reaching higher. The mental body is depicted by the square around the other two, as the mental body can think inside and outside of the box. Finally, the spiritual body is illustrated by the circle which encompasses all the other bodies. This masterpiece provides us with a model that reveals all four bodies in the same place at the same time.

What would it be like if all of the four bodies were in the same place and moving forward with each other? This sensation is much like love. When I am in love, my physical body desires to be around my beloved. My emotional body wishes to understand what my beloved is feeling. My mental body wants to listen to my beloved's thoughts and perceptions of the world around them. My spiritual body is soaring and dancing with the connection and love between both of us. When someone is in love, their physical, emotional, mental, and spiritual bodies are aligned. This is the sensation of being on your path. Love is the path.

I have met my soul walking along its path, when all my four bodies of existence are present. I listen to all four of my bodies, giving each of them a voice. This is when I know I am listening, and I give myself permission to experience the path below my feet on all levels. The compass is within each of us and can be experienced in many ways. Some feel it as a vibration of curiosity, some as an internal sense of knowing, some as a sensation of being led. Whichever way this is experienced, the common thread is that one is being directed by the *yes*, the sensation of being affirmed.

Of course, there is also the sensation of the *no*, the sensation of resistance. Without going too deeply into the comparing and contrasting of these two polarities, I will say the precise direction is a combination of balancing the yeses and readjusting through the nos. It can be a trade-off between the two in order to accurately direct our will and experience.

At times, we may struggle with figuring out our yes and our no. Here is a little trick to figuring out the *yes* from the *no* without confusing ourselves by overthinking it: general science reveals that we have approximately one hundred billion neurons in our brain.[10] Neurons are nerve cells that receive, process, and transmit information through electrical and chemical signals—our thinking cells, so to speak. Additionally, a human has approximately forty thousand neurons in the heart and four hundred to six hundred million neu-

---

10. Herculano-Houzel, "Human Brain."

rons in their gut.[11, 12] The brain is connecting and thinking, but so is the rest of the body—kinesthetic intellect. So, one can ask the body for its truth without the brain interfering and potentially overthinking the answer, but how?

✦✦✦ EXERCISE 4 ✦✦✦
Body Is a Pendulum

I invite you to stand up with your feet hip-width apart. Next, relax and ground into your feet and lower body without locking your knees or holding tension. As you relax within your body, say a true statement aloud. If the body agrees with the statement, it will lean slightly forward. Next, say a false statement aloud. If the body disagrees with the statement, it will lean slightly backward. Keep trying until you find your connection.

Keep in mind that if you make a statement and your body leans forward and backward, it is saying that there are truths and falsities within the statement that was made. Simply break down the statement into truthful parts and extract the non-truth. For example, if I were to say, "I am going to get a new job at ABC company" and my body slightly leaned forward followed by a slight lean backward, I would recognize that half of this statement is true and the other half is not. So, I would try it again: "I am going to get a new job." If my body slightly leaned forward, next I would say, "I am going to work at ABC company," and my body would lean backward. This would allow me to recognize that ABC company is not

---

11. Alshami, "Pain."

12. Kulkarni et al., "Advances in Enteric Neurobiology."

necessarily the company that my body senses that I am going to work for. Try this with everything, and listen to your body—it is speaking to you. Our physical bodies are nature; they are another way to connect beyond words.

The Medicine Wheel

The concept of working with a medicine wheel will assist us in balancing our lives. The medicine wheel can also assist us with holistically integrating the world around us with our unique lives. Medicine wheels can provide us with context and a center point that we can consciously return to when we feel out of balance with ourselves, our relationships, our career, or even our physical well-being.

The medicine wheel is also known as a sacred circle. It is hard to determine the origin of the medicine wheel. For example, the Navajo will work with this sacred circle as it gets handed down from generation to generation. The issue of historically tracing it back is that the Navajo were an oral culture until less than two hundred years ago. Our history was handed down through stories and storytellers. In these stories, language used around time was very loose. For example, "In the first world," "first man," and "first woman" were terms that indicated the creation story. If you ask me, I believe that the first type of medicine wheel was formed when tribes of humans gathered together and sat in a circle. Medicine wheels are circles, and circles are never-ending. One can energetically draw circles around almost anything. It's also like casting sacred space prior to doing ritual work or any sacred working. When you draw or cast a circle around anything, you are solidifying that which is within the circle and bringing your consciousness to it.

There is a concept in quantum physics called the observer effect. Simply put, the matter will change simply by being observed. In science and research, it is called the Hawthorne effect: a person who is being observed will act differently when they are aware that they are being observed.[13] The concept holds true in quantum physics; research energy changes based on the fact that it is being observed.[14] As I understand it, energy flows where consciousness goes. Hence, drawing a conscious circle around anything will change it and, for the most part, will hone what resides in the circle to become clearer to the observer.

In 2014, my husband and I planted ornamental ravenna grass around the periphery of our backyard. We planted eighteen stalks of raven grass that each stood about six to eight inches. Throughout that summer, I wanted to monitor and record the growth of the grass, so I picked one plant and took pictures of it every week or two to see how fast it would grow in order to compare it with where it started. Why not? It was fun. At the end of the summer, the stalk that I was monitoring and recording grew to be twice the size of the other ones, and it was the only stalk that plumed. What?! At this point, I realized that the natural world recognizes when it is being observed and may possibly even have an ego. Energy flows where consciousness goes. And encompassing anything with a circle—better yet, a medicine wheel—makes it stronger.

As we move through this book, we will be looking at many different populations within the natural world. Chapter 6, which focuses on the medicine wheel, will assist us in collecting all of these populations and placing them into a conscious circle. Through watching the cycles within the natural world, we will be able to understand

---

13. Fox, Brennan, and Chasen, "Clinical Estimation of Fetal Weight."

14. Weizmann Institute of Science, "Quantum Theory Demonstrated."

how this energy is assisting us. If we are aware of the energy and work with it in our day-to-day lives, we will be more successful. In chapter 6 we will also explore natural-world concepts of circles and cycles as well as the concept of building a medicine wheel. Finally, I will share my thoughts on how these concepts can be applied to relationships, business, and health.

The Shadow Side

The natural world can also assist us in doing shadow work. It can help us to recognize man-made judgments that cause us to deny our shadow side and it can help us to find the courage to face and embrace our shadow. But we must do so from a balanced position. This is the perfect time to introduce the concept of yin and yang.

Yin is represented by the dark swirl and yang is represented by the light swirl, each of which contains a dot of the other. This represents that everything contains the seed of its opposite. Just because these two are opposites doesn't indicate that there is a conflict between the two. It is very common within Western culture to think of light as good and dark (or shadow) as evil, but I invite you to take a step beyond that thought process. The yin becomes the yang and the yang becomes the yin. The day turns to night and the night turns to day. They flow in and out of each other. It is not about good destroying evil; it is about a system flow of opposites balancing. And so, it flows like the light and the dark within us, not to be confused with good versus evil.

Yin and Yang Symbol

The yin holds feminine energy and the yang holds masculine energy. Hence, if you destroy one, the other will cease to exist. In nature, we find many opposites; this is true within the laws of nature. The key is to live in balance and harmony with the world's point of view and to examine many perspectives. In chapter 7, we will explore concepts and ideas on how to become aware of your shadow and how to integrate this aspect of self. Additionally, chapter 7 will touch on how to approach the shadow, whether it is yours or someone else's. The day and the night, the light and the shadow, the yin and the yang: embrace the shadow or it will embrace you! I am excited to start delving into these concepts with you.

TWO
The Animal Kingdom

There are millions of animal species on earth at this point in history. They were here before mankind, and they can share their wisdom with us to assist and support us in our daily lives. When we examine the way each animal survives, hunts, mates, sleeps, and moves, we begin to learn from their wisdom and lifestyle. These lessons can be superimposed onto our personal relationships, our careers, and our health and well-being.

First, let's examine the way that the animal kingdom moves within the natural world. This is a way to categorize the basic animal kingdoms as taught to me by a Native American shaman. The four basic groups are:

1. **The Four-Legged.** As its name shares, it includes all animals with four legs that are mammals, such as cats, dogs, buffalo, wolves, horses, etc.

2. **The Winged Ones.** This includes all animals that can take to the air, such as eagles, hawks, owls, and crows.

3. **The Water Nation.** This group includes the animals which live in oceans, seas, lakes, streams, or any body of water. Some examples of these are whales and dolphins as well as small fish such as salmon. However, this group also includes other life-forms that live in the water, like otters and octopuses.

4. **The Creepy-Crawlies.** This group contains all insects, reptiles, and amphibians, including spiders, ants, snakes, and lizards. Note that a lizard has four legs but is not part of the four-legged group; this is because the lizard is a reptile, not a mammal.

Let's take a look at how each of these groups differs in how they move within the natural world.

The four-leggeds have all four feet on the ground and look at what is right in front of them. These animals represent the wisdom of being grounded and having a step-by-step process or structure; moreover, being practical and sure-footed in a situation. Additionally, these animals represent the ability to see what is right in front of you instead of imagining what is around the next corner. These are simple insights, but they are extremely helpful in many situations. If a four-legged shows up in our world, these are some of its messages: through its body language, it shows us how to move forward and how to approach a situation; it directly aligns us with the element of earth; grounded energy, stable energy, and steady energy; energy behaving as earth; and physical energy.

The winged ones can take flight. They have great vision, a bird's-eye view, which allows them to see the world from a higher point of view. These animals, by nature, are showing us how to rise above a situation. They also give us a different perspective in life. Look to see if a winged one is in flight or simply observing from a higher perspective. If they are in flight, it may be time to progress in a situation. If they are sitting and watching, it may be time to stop and take a look around before moving forward in life, or the winged one may be communicating that it is time to take a moment and think. Winged ones can directly align us with the element of air and mental energy. Thoughts fly through the air; they fly in and out of our consciousness.

The water nation is similar to the winged ones, but they flow within the water. Their movement comes from a deeper position. They may remain close to the surface, but some water nation creatures can go very deep and can withstand immense pressures. Some of them go with the flow, yet there are those who will swim against the current. All of these attributes can speak to us and give us additional insight into how we may want to move through any given situation. The water nation directly aligns with the element of water and emotional energy. This energy is ebbing and flowing, intensely deep, yet it can be clear and refreshing.

And, finally, the creepy-crawlies—the insects, reptiles, and amphibians. Although most of these are small in stature, this group holds many insights. Some creepy-crawlies travel in numbers, exhibiting teamwork and power in numbers. Others may be very territorial; loners who don't like to necessarily interact with others. Some of them are cold-blooded, not to be confused with an individual without emotions. Scientifically, a cold-blooded animal's internal temperature reflects the external environment. They can assist us in understanding our internal realm in relationship to our external environment. Creepy-crawlies can be found in every environment on Mother Earth and display the ability to adapt to environments and situations. These small creatures exhibit tenacity and patience. Seemingly unaware of their importance, they go about their tasks in nature and cultivate Mother Earth. There are some within this group that will go through a type of metamorphosis process—a transformative cycle. This wisdom can be very helpful to us when we are facing change within our life. Maybe we need to shed the old and step into the new; these little guys can show us how to do so naturally. The creepy-crawlies directly align us with the element of fire and spiritual energy. They can be very spirited, purifying, and inspirational.

Armed with just this information about the four basic groups, you could start communicating with the animal kingdom right now. However, there is so much more to unpack regarding each individual species and how they interact with the world. This is just a start for us to put on the lenses and peer into the animal kingdom to see what it is teaching us.

What's next? Let's examine the difference in how the animal kingdom may provide insight through hunting, mating, and sleeping. This will reveal a multitude of varying approaches for us to consider as we approach our own relationships, careers, and health.

When considering an animal, see how it obtains its food. This shows the different approaches we can take to gain and grow within different situations. There is more than one approach to feeding ourselves on a physical, mental, emotional, and spiritual level. On a physical level, some of us love to plan dinners and take time to cook and present a meal. Other times we may find ourselves visiting the drive-thru of a fast-food restaurant. On a mental level, sometimes we may find ourselves taking a deep educational course on any given topic. Other times, we may simply watch a short YouTube video in order to understand the broad strokes of a subject. On an emotional level, at times we may find ourselves reading or writing poetry with a loved one, or perhaps spending time with another to solidify the relationship. Other times, we may simply send a quick "I'm thinking about you" text to a loved one. On a spiritual level, at times we may find ourselves in a spiritual circle with others, practicing a long meditation, or enjoying a beautiful walk in nature to gain spiritual peace and perspective. Other times, we may simply read a short quote or an affirmation to connect to ourselves. Our approach to gain and grow on each of these levels may vary from slow and methodical to fast and everything in between. I am not suggesting that one way is better than another, I am simply presenting the plethora of ways we can feed our various bodies: physical, emotional, mental, and spiritual.

This, too, can be observed in the natural world. There are many different approaches. Some animals will move at a slow and steady pace to achieve food, such as a cow grazing in the field or a dog awaiting dinner. However, some animals hunt with ferocity, being very aggressive in their obtainment of food. Sometimes it's wise to pursue an opportunity and the best approach is to pounce on it. Take action and jump on an opportunity when it presents itself to you.

I recognize that pouncing on an opportunity may not be in everyone's nature. This may also depend on the situation. However, I would like to introduce the idea that the natural world recognizes that pouncing on prey is very natural—even sacred. There is a sacred relationship between the predator and the prey within nature. Barry Lopez says that a wolf may see a caribou one day but decide not to chase it; however, on another day, the two will lock eyes and their relationship within those moments will shift—

the caribou takes off running as the wolf pursues. Lopez describes the encounter as a ceremonial exchange: the flesh in exchange for respect for its spirit. They merge together. So is the circle of life.[15]

Some animals simply eat plants and show up to what seems like a buffet of food that is ready to be consumed. Remember, these animals may also need to store some food for the winter months. At times life may present a plethora of opportunities, choices, or ideas that are all ripe for the picking. This is a good time to pay attention and to store up some ideas for a later date. This is the time of plenty.

Some animals may lay a trap and lie in wait for the food to come to them. This situation holds the wisdom of being more strategic and understanding the pattern of what it is that you desire. Additionally, this situation requires preparation ahead of time and teaches observers to be patient with opportunities.

I am sure that there are many other ways that nature secures its food. Maybe you can come up with other ways and extract the wisdom for your own life. The point is that nature is communicating many different ways to approach gaining and growing. Find what works for you. Maybe one way works for your career and another way works better within a romantic relationship. There isn't one correct way—it all depends on the environment and situation.

How does each animal mate and/or connect in order to create? Some animals will mate for life; others will not. When we look at this, not only can we extract insights with regard to romantic endeavors, we can extract career insights as well. Maybe one person will approach a career path and connect with only that one career for the rest of their life whereas another person has multiple

---

15. Lopez, *Of Wolves and Men*, 61–62.

career paths within their lifetime. It is about what we connect with in order to create something.

Finally, let's consider together how different animals approach sleep and/or hibernation. My cat certainly likes her naps; however, she tends to sleep lightly for an extended amount of time versus deeply for a short amount of time. When we look at how different animals approach their sleep, we can compare it to our own personal habits. Some animals are nocturnal. Not only could we compare this to a person who is a night owl, but we could also say that the nighttime represents the unknown. Hence, an owl could denote a person who enjoys staying up at night and sleeping during the day, or it could denote an individual who is peering into the unknown or subconscious and can perceive what is there, such as a psychic.

Additionally, we should consider the color(s) of the animal. We can extract more of their teachings if we pay attention to this quality. For example, the beautiful colors of the magnificent peacock can be captivating, which is the point. The male peacock intends to distract us in order to divert our attention away from its mate and babies. What about the lessons of the chameleon? The chameleon will change its colors to match the environment that it is in. I guess the chameleon is nature's way of saying, "When in Rome, do as the Romans do."[16] It is another survival technique that we can see the wisdom in. There are times that it is best to simply blend in: the wise chameleon will disguise itself in order to hunt. Smart little character. The color of the animal may hold other messages; simply be aware and see what comes to you.

At this point, I hope that you are picking up what I am putting down: the concept that the animal kingdom holds wise insights

---

16. Speake, *Oxford Dictionary of Proverbs*, 78.

that we can consider and then apply to different situations in order to live a richer, more natural life. Take a moment and ask yourself what type of animal you emulate. For relationships, think about what type of animal the other person emulates. Are they grounded and steady? If so, they probably are behaving like some sort of four-legged. Are they up in the air, chatty, and constantly dreaming of the future? If so, they most likely are a winged one. Are they sensitive with a lot of feelings? They may be of the water nation. Are they transformative? If so, they may be of the creepy-crawlies. Relax and use your imagination; it will come to you.

Additionally, understand that people may change animals from one situation to another. Maybe they behave like a bear at home (responsible), but they are an otter at work (playful). Give yourself permission to explore this concept, and even to change your mind about what type of animal is in play. The more that you practice this, the easier it gets.

Animals come into our lives for a reason, a season, or a lifetime, much like we come in and out of each other's lives. When an animal comes in for a reason, it is here to show us how to move through a certain situation. If the animal comes in for a season, this animal will assist us for a time frame. When an animal comes to you for a lifetime, this is what is referred to as an animal totem. My ancestors taught me this; they learned it from their ancestors, who learned it from theirs, etc.

Another interesting concept is that my family clan has a shared totem—the totem of the bear. This was simply a fact that I grew up with and it wasn't to be questioned: the elders say it, it is true, and so it is. An animal totem is when you mirror the behavior of an animal within your life. There are many attributes that a bear can hold; I will share one. Some bears hibernate through the winter, and I have witnessed this within my personal life. Every now and again, I simply go within and enjoy time alone. This "hibernation" time provides me with introspection and helps me to ground and center myself. I have noticed that other family members tend to take quality time for themselves as well. After we have "hibernated," my family members reconnect and move forward in what seems to be a more collected style within our relationships and approach to the world. No matter what your totem animal is, you may interact with others and your surroundings just like that animal. It is natural.

✦✦✦ EXERCISE 5 ✦✦✦
Animal Totem

An individual does not have to know their actual totem to do this exercise; however, it does come in handy. So, how do we know our totem? There are many ways to discover and/or uncover your totem. I start by asking a person what their favorite animal is. This is a clue. The qualities and attributes that we admire within the animal kingdom usually are reflecting an aspect of our own personality. If an individual has many animals that they admire, this is where finding their totem can be a little tricky.

Another way to find your animal totem is to look around your house. Do you have a lot of pictures of horses or bears? Do you have figurines of eagles or hawks? This leads to another clue. Usually, people will surround themselves with their totem subconsciously, as the outside world will usually reflect the inner world. Especially if the individual creates or decorates their outside world!

Sometimes clues are in the physical appearance of an individual. Have you ever met someone with a haircut that looked birdlike, and they were visionaries and loved to chat? Chances are that they have a bird totem. The person who looks like a bear and is quiet but seems to know what is going on instinctively may have a bear totem.

Finally, an individual can go on a guided meditation to meet their animal totem. However, remember that animals can come into our world for a reason, season, or a lifetime. So, if you are going to do a guided meditation to find your totem, make sure that you intentionally go to meet your totem, or you may simply be meeting a reason or season animal. However you discover your totem is fine—at the end of the day, it is yours.

But let's say that you haven't found your totem yet, and you just want to understand a relationship better. Simply take a moment and ask yourself, *What animal am I behaving like in this relationship?* Then ask yourself, *What animal is the other person in this relationship behaving like?* Think about how those two animals coexist in nature.

Now we are going to apply some of these concepts from the animal kingdom to relationships and romance, business and finance, and health and well-being.

Relationships & Romance

In this section, we will be discussing all types of relationships, not just romantic relationships. Here we are going to open ourselves up to examining the different relationships within our lives. When you are looking at this from a romantic point of view, it will make sense just as well.

Different animals interact differently with those around them. Relationships and interaction in various situations are limitless. The key to relationships is to understand that others may be similar to you, but they will have their differences. Everyone is unique and because of this, we can see them and their nature through the lenses of the animal kingdom.

There is a story that I heard once. There are many variations to this story, but the point is still the same. It was about a snake who was cold and beginning to die. A young boy walked over to the snake and told him that he would take the snake to a warmer place if the snake did not bite him. The snake agreed, so the boy picked the snake up and carried it to a warmer place. The snake warmed up and bit the boy. The boy was shocked and shouted, "You promised that you wouldn't bite me!" The snake replied, "You knew I was a snake!" The snake didn't change its nature—it is what it is.

So it is with most people: our innate nature may not change. However, we may grow and mature, and some may change or adjust to life and its situations. It is a thought that you can play with if you wish. I am not suggesting that I know the answer to the question "Can people change?" I can only share with you what I have found—we can, but most do not.

Four-Leggeds in a Relationship

Keywords: grounded, realistic, steady, and down-to-earth

Let's take a look at four-leggeds within relationships. This energy can be interpreted as an individual who is very grounded within a relationship and may also be very stable (feet firmly on the ground). Depending on what type of animal, this person may want to be more independent, like a feline. They may prefer to mate for life, like a wolf. Some people need their alone time, like a bear who hibernates. Some people are social like herds of animals—they have their pack. It is good to be able to understand if you have (or are) a four-legged within a relationship. These people may not necessarily relate to the vision of the winged ones or the depth of the water nation. However, that doesn't mean that these types of people can't get along; their differences must be respected and understood.

My main totem is a crow (and raven), which is why I call myself Granddaughter Crow. The dark, iridescent feathers of a crow represent the mystery void, the place which all things come from and all things will return to. Some people are afraid of the mystery void. Some people are afraid of crows. Crows are messengers; they can stomach a lot. All of these traits are very useful in my relationships and career. My husband, however, is very much like a wolf. He sees what's right in front of us as I am looking at the big picture. He keeps us grounded. He is my protector.

Wolves and ravens have a symbiotic relationship within nature. The raven will rise above and see what food is in the forest. However, it is the wolf's job to hunt the food. Hence, the raven and the wolf will eat together. This is a good example of how two individuals can coexist by understanding which animal totem they have and how it works within the relationship. If I didn't respect his totem and tried to get him to behave exactly like me, it wouldn't work.

There are other examples of relationships within nature that allow us to understand why we may get along with some people and why it is more difficult to get along with others. Maybe it is natural to not like everyone that you meet. Maybe it is okay to not like someone for some unnamable reason and to simply keep a little more distance. However, if you are in a situation where you are unable to avoid this individual, at least you are able to understand their nature and respect them for that, even if you do not approve.

Winged Ones in a Relationship

Keywords: visionary, thoughtful, messengers, and big-picture thinkers

Winged ones within a relationship are individuals who rise above situations and see the bigger picture, the whole lay of the land. This is not to say that other animals do not, but it comes into view faster for winged ones. These people like to talk and share their messages with others; however, they might not necessarily be able to ground their energy as fast as a four-legged.

Winged ones may get flustered when it is too windy in the environment. They can soar with the wind, but too much confusion and rapid change may cause them to disappear until the environment calms down. Within relationships, they may tend to make big plans and fly directly to their goals. Depending on what type of winged one you are dealing with, they may move or think a little differently within relationships. A hummingbird will go straight for the nectar, the sweetness in life. An eagle may be able to ride those crazy wind currents. A dove may simply want to coo and experience peace.

Winged ones in a relationship may not necessarily understand or relate to the thought process of the four-leggeds. They may even think at times that the four-legged is moving too slowly and/or considering too many of the fine details. However, if they understand that they are working with a four-legged, it will improve the relationship.

When a winged one is in a relationship with a water nation person, they may relate to how that person moves within the world and what their flow is, be it in water or air. However, they may be looking at things from two different perspectives. This could serve the relationship well if it is understood.

A winged one being in a relationship with a creepy-crawly could be difficult, as many birds hunt and consume creepy-crawlies. This is the depiction of a relationship that seems one-sided, where one person takes and the other gives. I am not saying that this is right or wrong. It just is. If you are in this type of relationship, ask yourself if it is working for you. It may or may not be. The point is that this is a form of a relationship; however, once we become aware, there are questions that we must ask ourselves. *Does it work for me? Is this what I want?* Draw up the questions and take a walk, allowing the pure answers to rise within you.

Water Nation in a Relationship

Keywords: deep, fluid, feelers, and free-form

Now let's look at the water nation from the perspective of a relationship. Remember, the water nation is fluid and deep, and these individuals can be expansive within the subconscious mind and/or emotions. These people will potentially look for the depth within a relationship. They may want to work in teams, like a school of fish. They may want to approach life a bit more independently, like a shark. For the most part, the water nation will go with the flow; however, every once in a while, you may encounter a salmon—the one who goes against the current. If emotionally jolted, the water nation individuals may dive deep into the psychology of the situation—and potentially clam up or seem to disappear emotionally.

The water nation and the four-legged may have an interesting time getting on the same page. They will have to find common ground in order to connect—perhaps the beach. The beach is one of the landscapes where water meets the earth. Their relationship could get a little muddy at times; however, if they can respect and accept the other individual for what they bring to the relationship, it could be beautiful. Who doesn't enjoy a day at the beach?

As stated earlier, the water nation and the winged ones can work well together and potentially share many things in common.

The water nation and the creepy-crawlies can relate to each other as far as being a team and/or going solo. However, this relationship takes more time to understand each other as they could potentially be worlds apart.

Creepy-Crawlies in a Relationship

Keywords: transformative, adaptable, and work behind the scenes

Creepy-crawlies within a relationship can be transformative people, showing the other how to transform themselves. They also may be sensitive to the overarching environment of the relationship. They may tend to want to work in teams or enjoy big family functions, but not all of them will. Again, it depends on the type of creepy-crawly the person is. If the person is a butterfly, they know the process of the four stages of a project and how it looks different at every stage: the egg stage is the idea stage; the caterpillar stage is the research stage; the cocoon stage is a time to go within and consider what the end product will look like; the final stage is when the butterfly comes into manifestation. Hence, butterflies would get along with another creepy-crawly, a four-legged, and a winged one as well. Very transformative. On the other hand, the individual could be a spider: very creative, but please don't make them angry ... the bite could be poisonous.

Creepy-crawlies will get along with four-leggeds, as they both have experience with the ground and the world in front of them.

For example, the dragonfly would be considered a creepy-crawly. The dragonfly can symbolize the magical realm of metamorphosis. Depicted with iridescent wings, the dragonfly undertakes quite the metamorphosis during its life (first the egg stage, then larva / nymph, and finally the adult dragonfly). The dragonfly understands change. Let's say that this type of person is attracted to a buffalo. This may sound funny, but opposites do attract. The buffalo would bring great strength, abundance, and stability to the relationship, whereas the dragonfly would bring the ability to see into the magical / mystical side of life. Have you ever met a stable person with a partner who floats around in their own thoughts and ideas? The buffalo may be entertained by the dragonfly, and the dragonfly may need the stability of the buffalo.

Depending on what kind of creepy-crawly the person is, they might deeply understand a winged one and their great vision of the future. If the creepy-crawly has wings, a winged one and creepy-crawly could make a nice pair. However, as I stated before, some birds will consume creepy-crawlies. Simply be aware of these patterns. I can envision a butterfly making friends with a hawk: the butterfly stays low to the ground and stops to smell the flowers while the hawk shares the bigger picture with the butterfly.

A creepy-crawly and a member of the water nation could get along great, or they could be worlds apart. Creepy-crawlies will see the world and how to move around in it very differently than a member of the water nation. Think of an ant and a whale. An ant would share the minute details of daily life with the whale, while the whale would be able to explain the vastness of the bigger picture. As long as they recognize their differences, they could certainly enjoy this companionship.

Not all animals will get along with others—use your own judgment and know that this is a natural occurrence. Maybe you have good relationships, so allow this perspective to increase your understanding of how and why it is working. Maybe you are in a relationship that doesn't seem to work—allow this information to assist you in deciding how to make it work or maybe to move away from the relationship. The natural world is here to provide us with relationship insights, be they romantic or not.

Business & Finance

When we are applying animals to business and finance, we want to pay attention to the way that animal hunts and stores food. We also want to pay attention to how that animal moves within the world and what environments the animal will thrive in. In this section, I invite you to think about what type of animal you are with regard to business and finance as well as what type of animal you may want to work with in different business settings and/or your finances.

Four-Leggeds in Business

Keywords: process oriented, literal, and foundational

We have the bull and the bear markets within our economic system. The bull market is aggressively growing, and the bear market indicates when we should pull in and protect our investments. If you are in a situation where it would serve you to ground a project at work or within your financial situation, you may want to study a four-legged.

I enjoy working with the buffalo when it comes to careers. When the Native Americans would see the buffalo coming over the horizon, they knew that all of their needs would be met. They would soon have food, clothing, shelter, and tools. Every part of the buffalo became sacred to them. What is our buffalo in this society? Our career. Be mindful of your career, work with every aspect of it, and the buffalo will lead you to your abundance (even if that means switching it up).

Winged Ones in Business

Keywords: visionary, communicators, and grand ideas

If you find yourself in a situation where it would serve you to have great vision, start connecting with the winged ones. The winged ones are good to go to once a year to look at your career and financial situation via the big picture. The winged ones will show us an overview so that we can adjust ourselves and head in the direction that we wish to go. At times, we can get so caught up in day-to-day work that we forget the big picture and move off track from our big goals. It is ill-advised to have great vision without grounding that energy with a four-legged; this pairing allows you to manifest things here on Earth. We need to be grounded within the process in order for the great vision to come to fruition.

Water Nation in Business

Keywords: depth of processing, deep concentration, and deep
      thinkers

In our career, the water nation can assist us with going with the flow. It could assist us with understanding the depths and impact that we are making with our careers. When I think of finances, I observe money behaving like water—it flows from one thing to the next. However, it is good to build a dam every now and again so that it doesn't all flow away. The water nation can show us this.

Creepy-Crawlies in Business

Keywords: change agents, team player, and resourceful

Applying the creepy-crawlies to business and finance will lead to various messages and lessons depending on the type of creepy-crawly that it is. Adaptability to any situation is a part of their power. At times a creepy-crawly will want to work in large teams, such as any creepy-crawly that has a large community—ants, some beetles, bees, etc. However, there are some that are very territorial, such as most spiders. It is good to be aware of the spiders within the workplace.

Nature shows us how to respect the spider energy within situations. However, if you tend to be a spider within your career, choose a career that allows you to work more independently. Spiders have very creative energy, as they create webs wherever they go. These individuals may be musicians, artists, and writers. Respect their space and they will respect yours.

If you would like to learn how to save money, you may want to ask the bee. Bees seek out nectar from multiple resources and collect it and store it within the beehive. If you are worried about money, go sit in nature and see what animal comes to you. Figure out how this animal sustains itself throughout the year. The natural world is speaking with us constantly. It will speak louder if we listen and connect.

Additionally, once you find the animal that you are or wish to work with in business and finance, it is essential to pay attention to the environment where you place yourself. Is the environment conducive to your nature and your ability to grow? When I am speaking about the environment, I am suggesting that we look at the economy as a whole, the industry that you have chosen (or that has chosen you), and the culture of the workplace in which you work. Different animals will thrive in different environments. Ask yourself these questions: Are you in an environment where you are able to be yourself and thrive? Are you in an environment where you are stunted? Does the environment allow you to produce, or are you becoming an endangered species within that environment?

If you are a four-legged at work, such as a bear, wolf, or buffalo, you may be able to handle a colder environment. However, if you are a feline at work, you may wish for a warmer community to work with and can handle a junglelike environment. If you are a mouse at work, you are probably the type of person who notices tiny details that others may not catch; however, you may not be recognized for all that you do (and maybe you're okay with that). If you are a fox, you most likely blend into most environments, as foxes are found across the globe and their coat changes depending on the environment they dwell in. If you are in an environment that is not conducive to the type of animal you are and you are unable to change the situation at this current moment, you may want to draw upon an animal that can sustain itself in that environment and apply its wisdom in order to thrive. Use these insights until you move into an environment that you can naturally thrive in.

If you are a winged one at work, you are most likely a visionary. You have the ability to look at the big picture and assist with setting goals. However, I would suggest that you team up with a four-legged to make sure that your ideas will work well in the real world. Different birds will thrive in different environments, and some will fly south for winter. If you are a migrant bird within your career, you may like to change your setting every couple of years. If you are more of a tropical bird within your career, you may need to be in a warm setting with a workplace culture that is vibrant. Maybe you are a penguin and you like the frosty cool environment. Again, nature does not say that one way is right or wrong; it teaches us that each of us fits somewhere. Find your environment so that you can thrive naturally.

If you are a water nation at work, you may enjoy a free-form workplace, an environment that you can move freely within. If you are a salmon, maybe you enjoy working in a challenging environment or industry where you must move against the current. There are plenty of industries where this is possible. Let's say that you are a whale within your career; you really are a big fish in a big ocean and you have the ability to touch the depths and rise to the occasion. You may also have the ability to work within cooler environments and warmer workplaces. Maybe you are a tropical fish and you need a certain type of environment or you cannot survive. Work with these ideas and make the best choice for you.

If you are a creepy-crawly within your career, depending on what type of creepy-crawly you are, you may need a specific environment to work in. Maybe you are a worm and you like to unearth things. Maybe you are a lizard or a snake and you need a warm environment. If you are a lizard or a snake who needs a warm environment, please find this environment or you will grow cold inside, which is not healthy for you. Moreover, if you are an ant, you may need a teamwork environment with goals that only a community can reach together. Whatever your needs are, be aware of them and make your own choices.

Additionally, if you are a leader of a team, figure out what animal each of the team members is behaving like. It will serve the team well to be able to draw on each individual's strengths. It will also assist you in understanding who gets along with who and why as well as who is not getting along with others and why. This will ultimately produce a stronger team. Some individuals will want to work alone and in a quiet setting before they bring their progress back to the team, whereas others are motivated by connecting and working together. Neither is right or wrong; both are natural. The key is to become aware of a different perspective.

Another thing for leaders of a team to pay attention to is the workplace environment that they are managing. Become flexible with the environment. Note the ones who enjoy a cooler environment and let them work on their own for much of the time. Note the ones who enjoy a warmer environment and create situations where they can connect and communicate with their teammates. As leaders, we have such an impact on the seen and unseen workplace. We have the ability to create different environments for different people and situations. If you are enjoying this section, maybe you would like to have a team-building meeting where you ask each person what their favorite animal is like. Open up group dialogues on what this means to the group and how to respect each other. If you are not in an environment where you are able to freely do this, simply take note of each member and find a way to create an environment where each member is able to thrive.

There are multiple applications presented in this section, and the combinations are endless. Feel free to take time to adjust and readjust this information until it suits you well. Feel free to come up with your personal scenarios as the animal kingdom speaks with you. Remember, it may not speak in words, but it does speak volumes. I do hope that understanding our approach to business and finance through the wisdom and insights provided by the animal kingdom opens your eyes to new perspectives and approaches.

Health & Well-Being

When we are looking to the animal kingdom for messages around health and well-being, it is wise to consider how each animal takes care of themselves on a day-to-day basis. What foods do they eat?

How often do they rest? Are they nocturnal? How fast or slow do they move in the world? Are they seasonal? Do they hibernate or migrate to warmer climates at certain times of the year? When we align with an animal, we can take all of this into consideration and see how much applies to our current state of health and well-being. Below is an exercise which can shed even more light on this topic.

✦✦✦ EXERCISE 6 ✦✦✦
Diagnose the Four Bodies of Existence

When somebody comes to see me for healing, there are numerous ways I can begin. One way is very simple, and you can do this too: first, I pull out one of my favorite animal card decks and shuffle. If you do not have an animal deck, no worries. You can simply write the name of the animals on separate pieces of paper. I would recommend including animals from all four groups (four-legged, winged ones, water nation, creepy-crawlies). Here is a list of main animals and their keywords that you can draw from:

Four-Legged
- Wolf—finding their own way, teacher
- Bear—hibernation, inner knowing
- Horse—strong yet graceful, self-empowerment
- Turtle—slow and steady, Mother Earth
- Opossum—roll over and play dead, strategic
- Mouse—attention to detail, scrutiny

Winged Ones

- Eagle—connection with Great Spirit, rise above
- Hawk—keen observations, messenger
- Owl—look into the unknown, strong intuition
- Crow / Raven—magical (or a magical practice), the unknown
- Swan—gracefulness (or be gracious), purity
- Hummingbird—straight for the nectar, light and agile

Water Nation

- Whale—wisdom of history, go deep yet come up for air
- Dolphin—intelligent, community
- Otter—playful, creative female force
- Salmon—return to your place of origin, go against the current
- Octopus—mutable, diversion as a strategy to access a safer state
- Shark—strength, moving forward

Creepy-Crawlies

- Spider—creative, feminine energy
- Ant—teamwork, you can carry more than your weight
- Butterfly—transformational, light
- Lizard—sensitive, lose your tail (or tale) to protect yourself

- Dragonfly—illusions, transformation of emotional energy
- Alligator—take a big bite out of life, time to digest and rest

Secondly, I spread the cards out in front of the person facedown. At this point, I invite them to pull four cards and place them facedown in front of them. In this spread, each card represents one of the four bodies of existence. The first one is the physical body, the second one is the emotional body, the third one is the mental body, and the final card represents the spiritual body.

From their left to right, I turn the cards over (like turning the pages of a book). If the card is facing them, it indicates good health. If the card is facing away from them, it indicates the body that is looking for a little more attention. We turn the cards one by one and look to see if it is right side up or upside down before them.

I pay attention to the animal that is on each of these cards. This will give way to the rest of the information. When we are applying animals to health and well-being, pay close attention to that animal's diet, sleeping habits, and exercise level.

Remember the keywords for each of the animal groups. Four-leggeds tend to be grounded and steady. The winged ones tend to be light and visionary. The water nation tends to go with the flow and can get deep. The creepy-crawlies tend to show us adaptability and possibly transformation. When applying each of these to one of the four bodies of existence, they could mean a variety of things.

First Card—Physical Body

The card in the first position represents the person's physical body of existence. I look at what animal is indicated here and how that animal moves through the world. I look at what the animal eats and how often the animal sleeps. I also note how fast or slow the animal moves within its environment. For example, if it is a feline, I will recommend that the individual sit in one position until they recognize an opportunity; then they are able to pounce on it with ferocity. If it is a turtle, I will speak with the individual about moving slowly through life. Next, remember if the card is upright (facing them), this indicates good health and well-being. If it is reversed (facing away from them), this would indicate that their physical body needs more attention.

- If there is a four-legged in the physical position, it will indicate that they are moving in the physical realm in a step-by-step process. Look at what the animal eats, if it enjoys fruits and nuts or a lot of protein. All of this provides us with an additional thought process to consider. Again, looking at how fast or slow the animal moves through its environment will provide more insight into the individual. Some four-leggeds move very fast through their environment—this could indicate an agile person. If the card is upside down, it may indicate that they need to slow down and

move within the physical realm with one foot
in front of the other and not get ahead of themselves. Additionally, the person may need to
focus on eating more like the animal on the card
in a certain food group. Or the physical body
needs to ground and center; this could be something as obvious as going to see a chiropractor.

• If there is a winged one in the physical position,
it may indicate that this individual may want to
eat like a bird or stay light on their feet. Additionally, how does the winged one move through
its environment? Maybe it soars like an eagle,
flying high and solo, which could indicate that
the individual's physical body is strong and light.
Maybe the animal is a hummingbird and has the
ability to stay in one place, fly sideways, or fly
backward. This would suggest a very agile and
flexible physical state. If reversed, it could be
asking the person to physically slow down and
be observant of the environment, or it could be
stating that in the physical realm, this individual may feel as though their wings have been
clipped—possibly a current illness or surgery.
Take time to heal. If the hummingbird is reverse,
you may want to discuss their sugar levels, as the
hummingbird goes straight for the nectar and
sweetness. Whatever it is, look at the winged
one and allow it to communicate with you.

• If the animal is of the water nation, it could
indicate an individual who is going with the

flow of their day—the ability to move within the environment with ease. Recognize how the animal will move within their environment. If it is a crab, maybe sidestepping their day and slowing down is in order. However, if the animal is a shark, I would recommend continuous movement forward, as many sharks cannot breathe if they stop swimming. If the card is reversed, it could be asking the person to relax and physically go with the flow of their environment—they should not push too hard. Note what the animal likes to eat. You may even want to discuss bringing more omega-3 into their diet, as fish are rich in omega-3. There are many messages here. Extract the ones that resonate with you.

- If it is a creepy-crawly, it is revealing how this individual is moving through their day, whether that is within a team or solo. If it is a team creepy-crawly, it could indicate that the person would benefit from group exercise. Note what the animal eats and drinks and how they move physically in the world; this will lead toward a deeper understanding of what is recommended for them on a physical level. Reversed, the card could represent becoming more adaptable or more teamwork, or to go it alone (again, depending on which creepy-crawly it is).

Second Card—Emotional Body

Next is the emotional body card position. The emotional body represents how you feel about yourself and/or the world around you. Do you feel emotionally grounded, emotionally light and cheerful, emotionally fluid, or emotionally transformed? Let's take a look at the various interpretations that you can extract from each of the four animal kingdom groups.

- If there is a four-legged in the emotional position, it reveals a very emotionally grounded individual. Note how fast or slowly the animal moves within the world. If it is fast like a gazelle or a cheetah, it reveals how quickly the individual is able to process emotions. If the animal is a snail, it may recommend a slower processing of emotions. If the animal eats a lot, it could be suggesting an individual who has great emotional capacity. If the card is reversed, it could be asking this person to ground their emotions and breathe. If the animal eats a lot and the card is in reverse, it may be revealing an individual who is emotionally starving and needs positive emotional support.

- If there is a winged one in the emotional card position, this could be indicating an individual who considers the whole picture and understands others' emotions from a logical point of view and/or has the ability to rise above emotional situations. If the card is reversed, it is asking the individual to rise above an emotional situation and to depersonalize the situation. A reversed card could also mean that the individual could benefit from an environment where they are allowed to express their emotions freely and without retribution.

- If it is a water nation animal in this position, it could be speaking of an individual who has emotional depth. The individual is also sensitive to the environment and feels the waves of the emotions of those around them. Emotions are like water; they ebb and flow. If the card is reversed, it is asking the individual not to drown in their emotions and to come up for air. We need proper environments where we are able to process all of our emotions.

- If there is a creepy-crawly in this position, it could indicate an individual who is emotionally adaptable to situations and potentially offers emotional support to others. If reversed, we are looking at an individual who may need more emotional support from others or may need to be a little more emotionally adaptable. If it is a reverse spider, for example, it could indicate that we are creating situations from a negative position, and we need to rest before we speak.

Third Card—Mental Body

Now let's look at the mental body card position. The mental body aligns us with our thoughts and mental capacity at this point in our lives. It has everything to do with the mind and the brain. Aligning the mental body with the four animal groups can provide us with deeper understanding of how an individual may be processing the world around them. Let's take a look at some of the things it can reveal.

- If there is a four-legged in this position, it indicates someone who knows how to mentally create a step-by-step process which will lead to the end goal. This is an individual who is grounded and solid within their thinking and has a process and a plan to move forward in their life. If the card is reversed, it may be asking the individual to meditate and to slow down their mind instead of getting ahead of themselves. A reversed card can also suggest that something happened in this person's life that may have unearthed them—a rapid change of plan or unexpected information came to them. This individual may need to take some time to reposition their thinking in order to move forward.

- If there is a winged one in the mental body card position, this is an individual who is visualizing the big picture and can mentally fly straight to where they want to go without fetter. There is a sense of freedom within their thinking. This is an individual who can rise above situations and entertain a lot of different thoughts without getting tired. If it is upside down, this individual may be mentally spun around and unable to see the big picture. The reversed card could also hold a sensation of being let down by a conversation or some form of communication. I would recommend listening to this individual so that they can find the wind under their ideas once again.

- If the water nation is in the mental body position, it reveals an individual who is taking other people's emotions into consideration before they make a decision. It could also reveal an individual who is a psychologist or someone who moves into the depths of one's mind. If the card is upside down, the individual may want to take other peoples' emotions into consideration before making a decision or seek counsel in order to lighten up their thoughts.

- If a creepy-crawly is in the mental body, it could indicate an individual who is considerate of others and/or one who thinks for themselves (depending on the type of animal and the way it moves within the natural world). If the card is in a reversed position, this would indicate that the individual may want to look at a group perspective before making a decision, or that the individual may need to think for themselves (team versus individuality).

Fourth Card—Spiritual Body

Finally, let's look at the spiritual body card position. This position could represent your spirituality or how spirited you might be. Let's take a look at what the four main animal groups look like within the spiritual body.

- If there is a four-legged in this position, it indicates an individual who is grounded spiritually and who is steadily moving forward. It may also indicate an individual who remains grounded in life, even when drama happens. If reversed, this would indicate an individual who may need to ground and center spiritually. Something may have happened that has them questioning their spiritual belief system, or something happened that made them loose steam (spirit) in the direction that they were headed.

- If there is a winged one in this position, it can indicate a spiritual messenger who sees the big picture. It could also indicate a light, happy, cheerful individual that gets us moving again: someone that champions for others. If reversed, this could indicate that the individual is not listening to the spiritual message and / or they have lost sight. Additionally, it could indicate that a once lighthearted person is experiencing a difficult time and is less spirited than they normally are.

- If there is an animal from the water nation in this position, it could indicate someone who has much spiritual depth or an individual that is a spiritual counselor or healer. If the water nation card is upside down, this could indicate that the individual may need a break and is overwhelmed spiritually. The individual could benefit from spiritual counseling or support—remember, the water nation goes beneath the surface and into the depths.

- If there is a creepy-crawly within this position, this individual is adaptable to spiritual ideas and concepts. Additionally, this individual is a manifester and has tapped into their creative side in order to manifest. It could also indicate an individual who enjoys being a part of a spiritual group. If the card is reversed, this could indicate that the individual could benefit from a new spiritual perspective and/or a spiritual group.

These are simply starting points to begin to move into a more in-depth notion of where a person is within their health and well-being. This, again, comes from the concept that health and well-being have to do with the balancing of the physical body, the emotional body, the mental body, and the spiritual body. Once we begin to understand each of these and how they relate to each other, we begin to see the totality of the whole person and we can grow, feed, rest, and exercise ourselves holistically. There is more information on the holistic aspects of balancing ourselves in chapter 6.

THREE
The Plant Kingdom

The plant kingdom is alive. Scientific research continues to study how long the plant kingdom has been here on Mother Earth, but it has been millions of years. Plants were here before animals and before the human race; they are our eldest teachers. What other organism has survived so long and still produces life force simply by its presence? Just like the animal kingdom, the plant kingdom reveals many messages to us without speaking a word. It teaches us to pay attention to our environment, to identify our purpose and functionalities within any given situation, and how to grow into our authentic self. It reveals to us that there are many ways to grow and many directions to grow in. There are different heights to achieve and different functions to be done in order to be a part of something greater than ourselves—to be a part of a biosphere.

The plant kingdom provides me with a sense of belonging. A traditional medicine person is tied into the rhythms and forces within nature and the world around them. They hold the ability to see the visible and invisible world around themselves.[17] These individuals hold an understanding of the concept of animism. Animism is a worldview which states that everything has consciousness; moreover, that everything has a soul. Without getting too philosophical about the term or definition of the word *soul*, I will simply state that all is energy, and energy holds consciousness. On one level or another, all things have an awareness.

All is energy—this is physics. Physics tells us that everything that is matter is made up of atoms. All is energy. There is no separation between the field of matter and the energetic field at a fundamental level. All energy holds some form of consciousness—hence, everything holds consciousness. Maybe this is what the traditional medicine person understood, prior to what quantum physics explains to us now. We can study and play within the realms of science—and I hope that we continue to do so—however, please do not let your thoughts get so complex that you forget the basics of what you know. Listen to your intuition. What do you know? What do the trees know? What is their wisdom?

Plants have taught me many things. One thing is that humans are the only organisms on the face of this earth that try to justify our existence—plants and animals simply don't question who and what they are. Plants will grow into their greatest sense of self, but people limit themselves for one reason or another. I asked the tree, "What gives you the right to be here and to grow so tall and strong? Don't you fear what other plants will say about you?" The tree just waved at me as if to say, "Be more flexible with yourself.

---

17. Andrews, *Animal Speak*, 1.

Don't compare yourself with others. Simply be the best that you can be." I love plants; they are some of my greatest guides.

I am going to invite you to examine the world around you from this perspective. When one subscribes to the worldview of animism, it may change the way that they interact with the world around them. They may give more respect to the world around them or become more conscious of the world's rhythm and forces. This concept of animism opens us up to considering that nature is aware that we are here too: when I touch a tree, the tree is touching me back. The earth is aware that I am here—it senses my feet as I walk upon it.

The tree doesn't look at the rosebush and say, "You're not tall enough, so you're not good enough." Likewise, the rosebush doesn't look at the tree and say, "Well, I'm prettier than you are, and I smell of sweet romantic essence." The natural world doesn't have the types of arguments that humans do. The natural world shows us that we each get to grow into our authenticity and greatness, even when it differs from another's. Moreover, the plant kingdom assists others to grow into their authenticity. Plants work well with other plants; they create a natural biosphere when placed beside one another.

Everything is continuously communicating with itself and its surroundings, but how it communicates is not necessarily verbal. Sometimes communication occurs via scent. So, how does the natural world communicate in scent? And do we communicate with scent too? Yes! One way that humans communicate via scent is with special cologne and perfumes in order to attract those around us. Another example of communication via scent is when we burn a scented candle or incense so that it will change the mood of our environment.

The tomato plant can communicate with other tomato plants, caterpillars, and wasps by releasing a scent. In order to communicate with other tomato plants, one plant will excrete the scent called methyl jasmonate—this is a common chemical used within the perfume and cologne industries. For a tomato plant, this chemical signals other plants to be on heightened alert, signaling that the plants are under attack. The plant can recognize who the attacker is by recognizing the insect's saliva. If the insect is a caterpillar, the tomato plant will excrete a fragrance that attracts parasitic wasps to attach to the caterpillar. Similarly, when apple trees are under attack from caterpillars, they send out a fragrance to some birds, which come to the tree's defense.[18]

Another interesting thing that researchers have found is that after a plant emits scents for the first time, it is able to somehow remember what it did and emit these scents faster the next time the plant is under attack, meaning that plants can remember and learn as they grow. The intelligence of the plant kingdom is awesome. Further research shows that all plants can communicate through scent—they can warn each other of a coming danger, allure beneficial insects, send out SOS signals to allies, and even coordinate amongst themselves. No wonder gardens smell so alive—scent is the way that plants communicate![19]

Another example of a plant learning and changing within its evolution and cultivation is the honey locust. Thousands of years ago, this tree had big thorns and thistles on it in order to detract woolly mammoths from partaking in its delicious foliage. Nowadays, in a world without the woolly mammoth, this defense mech-

---

18. Koechlin, *Plant Whispers.*

19. Koechlin, "Tomatoes Talk, Birch Trees Learn."

anism is no longer required; hence, these thorns have been culti-vated out of the tree, which is common in today's landscapes.[20]

The natural world is constantly evolving with the current state of events. We would be wise to do the same. For example, I am not in the same environment that I was when I was younger. I have different relationships, so I may take a lesson from the honey locust and drop some of my old defense mechanisms in order to relate to the world around me as it is now.

Plants communicate above- and underground. There is a whole intercommunication underneath the ground. At times they are exchanging nurturance; other times they are sending out signals that will detour nearby plants. I think that science is merely scratching the surface when it comes to how plants can communicate under-ground—pun intended. Now that you know about plant commu-nication, a walk in the forest will become even more meaningful. The plant kingdom is aware of us as we move through the forest. I wonder what is it saying?

If you think about fairy tales, you might notice that there are magical forests in many of the stories. Some are forbidden forests, some are haunted, some are full of life and wonder, and some are enchanted. Perhaps we can now understand what our elders were sharing with us by including so many forests in their stories: the combination and communication of the plants.

Moreover, we could certainly learn lessons on resourcefulness and sustainability from the plant kingdom. Most plants will make their own food via photosynthesis. Let's step back for a moment—remember grade-school science class? Photosynthesis is the pro-cess in which plants make their own food in order to grow and develop. For this process, they require various elements: sunlight,

---

20. Boggs, "Honeylocusts and Mastodons."

carbon dioxide, water, and chlorophyll (the green within the plant). Through the roots, most plants will receive minerals and water from the soil and send it up through the stem to the leaves. On the leaves, most plants have tiny pores called stomata. Through these pores, the plant draws in carbon dioxide from the environment. When the sunlight touches the leaves, it works with the minerals, water, carbon dioxide, and chlorophyll to provide the plant with nutrients. From this, the plant will emit oxygen for us to breathe. We inhale oxygen and exhale carbon dioxide. Without plants, everything that requires oxygen would cease to exist. Plants are essential to all life forces on Mother Earth. They can produce their own food, give us oxygen, and feed us as well. With this understanding in mind, I say that plants are our eldest wisdom keeper.

I wonder what lessons we can learn from photosynthesis. What lessons come into your mind? I think about drawing upon the energy that you need in order to grow, combining this energy with what you have, and bringing this into the light of day in order to produce self-sustaining energy as well as enough energy to share with others. In short, that is what photosynthesis shows us. You can begin to apply this one lesson to your life, your relationships, your career, and your health. Be your greatness!

Plants were here before us, and they will be here after us. The ancient and indigenous people learned to work with plants from the heart of the world, from the plant itself.[21] They insisted that plants can speak to humans, if only humans would listen and respond to them in the proper state of mind. As I was growing and learning about spiritual concepts and how they are brought to us through the natural world, I wondered who taught my ancestors how to work with the sacred earth for healing. In the Navajo tra-

---

21. Buhner, *Secret Teachings of Plants*, 2.

dition, it is common to visit a peyote medicine person for a sacred ceremony.

One night, I had a dream. I dreamed that I was sitting in a sacred circle around a fire with my ancestors. There was a medicine man there. He began to speak to me. He said, "One day, when I was a young man, I was standing on a hill. The wind changed, and so I followed it. When the wind stopped, I stopped, and that is when I found a little plant. It was the peyote that taught me how to work with it."

I woke up and wrote down the details of my dream. It was amazing! *Is this how we can communicate with the natural world?* I wondered. *The plant was the teacher.* I wonder, if we were silent enough, if we could remember how to learn from plants—how to learn from the natural world—again. I believe that all of our ancestors, all across the globe, knew how to do this in one way or another.

There are many ways to look at plants as bringers of wisdom. If you are well studied in the plant kingdom, I encourage you to extract all of the metaphors that plants teach us and grow with these lessons. If you are like me, you may not know the scientific name for all the plants, but you can still learn from them. Each plant has an environmental preference and varying characteristics that make it unique. Different plants show us different things.

For example, what if you were to superimpose the plant kingdom onto the human race? What would you discover? You may find that some people are like trees: they grow tall and strong; they provide shade and housing for others. Some people are like rosebushes: they are beautiful and smell wonderful, but their protective thorns might getcha. Some people are like cacti: pretty from a distance, but don't hug a cactus.

Superimposing the plant kingdom onto the human race helps us realize that we are not all supposed to be the same, yet we all have a perfect environment. Not everyone grows tall like the trees, but we are beautiful in our own regard and for our own purpose. And at times, someone will be a cactus—this is natural, not personal. Certain people grow in certain environments, whereas others would not be able to thrive in such an environment.

Relationships & Romance

The natural world is constantly finding its balance. Within the plant kingdom, we need to become aware of environment. Different plants will grow and thrive in different climates, and so it is with relationships. Additionally, many plants hold a symbiotic relationship with each other.

I want to start this section by sharing a nice story about the symbiotic nature of some plant life. Let's start with the legend of the three sisters. The three sisters represent beans, squash, and corn. The littlest sister wore green; she was so young that she could only crawl (beans). The middle sister wore yellow, and she had a way of running off chasing the sun and the wind (squash). The eldest sister wore a pale green shawl and had yellow hair that would blow in the wind (corn); she stood tall and watched over her younger sisters.

These crops are sisters because, if planted together, they complement each other in their growth and development. They all become stronger as a result of their relationship; however, they grow differently. This is much like our relationship with each other! Although we are different in stature, the way we dress, and what we bring to the table, we all can assist each other in strengthening our individual authenticity.

When corn is planted, it provides a natural trellis for the beanstalks. Together the corn and beans provide shade for the squash to grow. In exchange, the squash will grow low and wide, keeping the soil shaded and moist for the corn and beans. Beans provide nitrogen to the soil, which assists both the corn and squash. Low-lying squash also help against the establishment of weeds, and the prickly hairs of the vine will help detour pests. Beans, squash, and corn work together and grow stronger because of their relationship.

And so it is with humans when we find the right friendships and relationships. Have you ever been placed in a position of leadership and felt as though others were growing because of you? Please don't push them away. Be their corn! Have you ever grown out of someone's success? Thank them for being your corn—or maybe just send them a greeting card, as they may not understand what you mean. Do you feel as though everyone else is growing tall in their successes, but you are simply holding space for them to grow? Be their squash! I have found that I have been other people's corn, beans, and squash. Each of these positions is necessary and helps someone else. Let's celebrate our differences and rejoice in our authenticity. I appreciate what everyone brings to the table—the variety is tasty!

Let's take a look at trees for a moment. There are many human similarities to trees. Trees are tall and strong; some people are tall and strong in stature or in spirit. Trees provide homes for many small animals; some of us wish to hold a protective, safe place for others. Many trees provide shade perfect for rest or a picnic; some people enjoy creating a space for others to relax or rejuvenate. Many trees bear fruit or nuts for us to eat; some people like to provide for others. Some may be poisonous, like the yew tree; some people may speak in poisonous words—steer clear and try not to take the yew tree personally.

Some trees are evergreens; they remain lifelike throughout every season. This could depict an individual who seems to bring positive life force to any given situation—forever the color of life, green. These trees have the ability to thrive in cooler environments and are even a part of the holiday season at the end of the year in some cultures. Now, let's consider a palm tree. These are trees that grow very tall, yet they require a warm, tropical type of environment in order to grow. What if I was a palm tree and I was in a relationship with an evergreen? I would have to recognize that I may require a lot of compassion and warm smiles, maybe even words of encouragement, in order to grow and thrive. However, the other person may not necessarily require all of those things because they handle a colder environment with ease—they might even prefer it! However, there are some evergreens that thrive within warmer environments as well.

The more specific you can get, the more insight you will have into a relationship. If you or someone around you seems to identify with a certain type of tree, study the tree and its traits in order to gain more insight into that individual's character and purpose.

There are other types of plants too. Let's take a look at flowers. Flowers are known for their beauty, both in shape and in fragrance. They are often welcomed as a method of showing love, healing, or friendship. Some people are like this as well: this is the type of individual who is seen as gracious and kind, an individual who lights up the room when they arrive. This type of individual may tend to be a little gentler and/or sensitive. They may not stay around for a long time, but they welcome us, refresh us, and make us smile.

I have a lot of relationships in my life. At times, I may mistake a relationship as a long-term tree relationship rather than a flower. The key is to pay attention to the relationship and to respect it for what it is and for how long it lasts. Flower relationships can be beautiful, but allow them to naturally come in and out of your life with beauty.

Other individuals may be like the beans within the legend of the three sisters. These individuals may stay low to the ground and will need some support in order to climb to the sky. This is fine as long as they have other plants to give them support; however, keep an eye on the vine so that it doesn't take over and choke out other life-forms. A lot of times, individuals who are of service will come across vines. The individual will provide support and lift up the vine-like person; this is lovely, but it can be taken advantage of. Please be aware of this phenomenon and set healthy boundaries so that you, as a person of service, do not get overwhelmed. Remember, some vines produce fruit for others, such as beans or grapes or melons. So, if you are a person of service, take note of what benefits the other person is bringing to the world and encourage this behavior.

There are many types of plants beyond trees and flowers. There are vegetable gardens and plenty of fruits. Think of all of the beauty that your favorite plants bring to you. What is your favorite flower? What is your favorite fruit or vegetable, and how does it grow? As much fun as it is to focus on the fruitful plants that surround us, we must also be aware that some people are like weeds.

Weeds do have a place within the world. My husband says that a weed is merely a plant that is growing outside of its intended environment. For example, wildflowers are beautiful and fragrant; however, they are not welcomed in a well-manicured tomato garden. Pay attention to your garden of friends and family. Make sure you recognize a weed when it arises and take action accordingly. If someone is sucking the life force out of a group, maybe that individual simply needs to find a different environment to grow in. I'm not trying to hate on weeds; rather, the natural world is showing us this effect so that we are able to understand how to navigate our lives.

✛✛✛ EXERCISE 7 ✛✛✛
Plant Totem

Consider the following question: "If I were a plant, what type of plant would I be?" Think about how the plant grows—does it grow quickly or slowly? What are the characteristics of the plant and the functionality that it may have? What environment does it thrive in? In what environment can it not sustain itself? These are very helpful clues to uncover your personality and what you need to succeed.

Next, consider what type of plants others are behaving like and what environment they can thrive in. There are so many possibilities.

I believe that every human being has a place within this world. Finding the environment that is the most conducive to your growth is one of the messages that the plant kingdom provides—when you find your environment, you will find others who understand you. Together, we can all grow with purpose and meaning. My husband says that soulmates always find each other because they are drawn to the same spaces. If you are looking for a meaningful relationship, go out and do what you enjoy doing! You never know … lightning might strike.

When you look to the plant kingdom for more insight on yourself and others from a relationship point of view, consider the following things. What type of plant are you? What type of plant is the other person? Pay attention to the characteristics and the functions that the plant will have in order to gain wisdom about the relationship and what the product of the relationship is. Additionally, consider the environment that each plant will thrive within: Is it warm or cold? Dry or wet? How much sunshine and attention does it need in order to grow? Finally, remember that you may grow differently with each relationship that you have. You may be someone's tree, strong and stable. You may be someone's flower, bright and cheerful. You may even be someone's weed. All types of relationships are revealed to us in the natural world.

Business & Finance

One day my son called me up after work. He was confused. He shared with me that he was upset because his colleagues at work were yelling at him and picking on him. Apparently, my son works hard whether or not he is being supervised. He was working with others who only worked when the boss came around, getting the minimum done. His colleagues told him to slow down and that he was making them look bad by getting so much work done. My son was confused because he thought he was hired to work hard, but his colleagues were relaying the opposite message. He was young, so he didn't know if he should be working hard or trying to become a part of the group. I've been there.

I said, "Michael, you are a tree. They are bushes. As a tree, you will grow tall and strong and outgrow your current position. They are bushes, so they are not looking to grow tall and strong in the company. But a bush is a bush. They grow shorter than a tree, but they do cover the ground."

My son stopped trying to fit in at work and he began to grow tall like a tree. I believe that he is a leader, and one of the things that is helpful for a leader to learn or know is what is happening when you are not in the room. Now he will detect who is a tree and who is a bush. It is what it is.

When we are looking at the area of business and finance and finding the wisdom of the plant kingdom, there are many approaches. What type of plant are you? This approach allows you to understand what functionality you wish to have within your career and what environment you grow best in. This helps with finding purpose within your career. For example, if I know that I am a fruit-bearing tree, I may look for a nice orchard to grow in. The application here could be seen in a group of individuals who are self-sustaining yet produce similar outcomes. We see this with a group of lawyers who come together under one roof; each of them has their own clients, yet they are houses in a firm. We also see this in the healing industry, where a group of professionals each have their own clients yet share a common space. Even a yearly convention, held within one large facility yet with many different entrepreneurs all providing their goods or services, illustrates this point.

Let's go back to the story of the three sisters and apply that concept here. Maybe you are corn, or beans, or squash, and you are looking for the other two in order to thrive. When you apply this concept to business, you understand the model of working with others who have different talents in order to grow or thrive. An example of this would be what you find at the local gym: work-out equipment, a personal trainer or teacher, and maybe even a massage therapist—all three in one. Another example is a team of individuals who each have their own niche who come together to produce something larger than what they could offer individually.

The type of plant that you are within a business will allow you to find the right place in order to grow. When we are speaking about finances, we can apply the same insights here. Look at your finances like they are seeds. Depending on the reality of your personal situation, your finances may be like corn, beans, or squash seeds, or maybe you're blessed and you have the seeds to grow trees. Now, think about placing your finances into an environment that they can grow and thrive in. Maybe it is an interest-bearing savings account for starters. Next, once you grow that to a certain level, you can take part of that and place it into a CD or invest it in the market, etc. Here is the wisdom: plant your finances where they will grow.

Timing is key as well. If I only have a little bit of extra finances, I need to be mindful of when I invest it into the markets—if it is a risky investment, my finances may grow faster. On the other hand, I may lose everything at a moment's notice. Maybe I am willing to do this when I am young and have plenty of time to make more; however, if I am older, I may consider a slower-growing investment which will have a lot less risk to it.

As I stated earlier, there are many ways to apply the wisdom of the plant kingdom to our career and finances. In addition to asking what type of plant you are, maybe you could ask, "What type of plants do I wish to grow?" In other words, what product or service do you wish to offer? This question can open up a lot more ideas to extract when approaching business. Do you enjoy growing something fast and gaining quickly? Or do you prefer smaller profits but more products or services?

Do you enjoy working for a long time on something large and seeing the results in a few years? Now we are looking at a whole different set of characteristics. If this is more your speed, you may want to look to the trees for insight and wisdom, as it takes years to grow a tree; however, the end result is strong and stable and will be around for a long time. If you like to grow a tree, allow yourself the time it takes to develop. You may also need to secure resources to support the growth, as the tree will not bear fruit for the first few years, but after that, it takes little work and still yields fruit (or finances).

When you grow in business, whether you work for an organization or are an entrepreneur, it is helpful to understand what type of plant you are growing. Personally, I am an entrepreneur. It has taken several years for me to continue to gain and grow, just as it takes time to grow a tree. At times, I must direct or redirect my growth process—trim a little here and prune a little there. However, in the beginning, I knew that I was growing a tree, so I gave myself time to grow and resisted frustration.

Some are a part of an industry that grows like a weed—fast and furious, yet shallow in its root system. This type of industry moves in fast and moves out fast—not a lot of sustainability. These are those "get rich fast" businesses. These types of businesses will drain the garden (your bank account). Please be watchful of these and understand the nature of the weed. Yes, they can be green and full of life; however, be advised that if they are not monitored, they can take over the rest of your financial field.

If you are in a leadership position, it may be helpful to understand the environment that you are creating and hire individuals who will thrive within that environment. As a leader, you can have a great effect on the culture (climate) of your garden. Also, be aware of the individuals who are trees and nurture them in the way that allows growth. Trees will most likely be the individuals who will be taking over next—show them how to do this, please. Additionally, you may be leading some flowers, the cheerful people who enjoy decorating the office and enjoy being on a party-planning committee. They bring brightness to the environment. Maybe you recognize the team of three sisters; place these individuals together and watch them all grow. Whatever it is, recognize that you are overlooking a garden, and nurture the garden in accordance.

The plant kingdom holds the wisdom to all business environments and financial streams. Look at what you like to grow and find a plant that emulates this growth process. This simple concept can allow for outside-the-box thinking, a variety of approaches, and even epiphanies to your world. The wisdom of the plant kingdom is a perfect model to grow your career and/or finances.

Health & Well-Being

I am hoping that by this point you are generating your own perspectives of how to apply the wisdom of the plant kingdom to your life. It is simply becoming aware of the way that plants grow, the environment that they thrive in, the functions and characteristics they hold, and how they work with each other. Now, let's analyze their wise insights into health and well-being. There are many ways to do this; we can look at how they live and adopt these concepts to live a more natural life, and we can also look at the medicinal purposes of fruits, vegetables, and herbs.

I used to be a jogger. Every morning I was up at four o'clock. Without even a thought, my running shoes were on and I was out the door. It is safe to say that I woke up as I was running. Those were much younger days for me, but I can still feel the warm breeze on my face and the sound of that same breeze moving the leaves on the trees around me. The world was quiet that early in the morning, and I would have the trees all to myself for an hour.

During the spring months, I would watch the budding leaves as if to say hello. In the summer months, I would listen to the leaves wave and chat with me. And then something happened one morning in autumn. As I was jogging, I noticed that the tree trunks looked like the human spinal cord, and the branches were the neural pathway within the mind. The neural pathways in the minds are thinking pathways, connecting one thought to another. Finally, a breeze came, and the magical tree released some leaves that danced happily down the road without a care in the world. It was as if to show me that there is a time for thoughts and ideas to bud and for them to grow, and that letting go of an idea can be easy, like the tree releasing its leaves. New thoughts will be buds soon. I suppose that I was under the impression that letting go of thoughts should be hard, but the tree taught me otherwise.

When approaching the idea of wellness, I reflect back on the concepts of the four bodies of existence—the physical body, the mental body, the emotional body, and the spiritual body. Each one of these bodies requires us to pay attention to them so that they are able to be healthy. This is like a garden to me. My physical body may require certain attention and nourishment, whereas my other bodies may require different types of attention and nourishment. I am a garden. I would like to reflect on the tale of the three sisters again here. What would it be like to physically sit still and align one of your bodies to corn, another to beans, and another to squash? Whichever one you choose to be can be telling in itself. Maybe your spirit is strong and tall like corn, your mind is holding space like squash, and your emotions begin to rise up and grow into the next expression of self? All is energy, be it physical, mental, emotional, or spiritual. Energy likes to be free to express itself. In this exercise, be mindful of who you are, where you are, what you feel, and what you desire.

When people discuss health and well-being, I think there is more of an intense focus on self rather than on relationships or careers. So, it is time to go within and discover. Play with the concepts and ideas that might be organically coming to you—I believe that we are remembering how to apply the wisdom and insights of the natural world back into our daily lives.

Trees can show us how to stand up for ourselves in all four bodies. They can also show us how to look at the bigger picture from a height perspective, as well as longevity. The trees teach us how to bend within the wind—to be flexible. The tree that does not bend in the wind will snap. The tree gains its strength as a result of the wind moving it. Trees teach us how to ground ourselves, draw upon inner resources, and connect with others. On a physical level, they show us how to stretch and how to be grounded and strong. On an emotional, mental, and spiritual level, trees teach us these things as well. In fact, there is a whole Celtic alphabet based on trees—it is called ogham. Each of the letters of this alphabet has a correlating tree. This is one example of how deeply connected to the plant kingdom our ancestors were.

Flowers can show you how to be graceful and gracious. They send good scents into the air. Obviously, on a physical level, this would be a nice smelling soap or shampoo or cologne. Additionally, this could represent a nice meditative or calming incense to relax your mind, calm your emotions, and lighten your spirit. Flowers are also very gentle, so this application works well for each of the bodies. Additionally, the flower demonstrates how to be open to working with others, as flowers need to be pollinated by bees in order to grow. Flowers bring joy and messages of health and well-being, such as sending "get well soon" flowers to another person. For the most part, flowers are seasonal, so this is a good reminder to take the time to stop and smell the roses for health and well-being in all of the four bodies of existence.

Maybe you feel like a vine in one or all of your four bodies; this is fine. Just go find a support system. This could be a physical therapist or a healer of sorts. On an emotional level, this could be a good friend or pet. On a mental level, this could be good counsel or someone to speak with and confide in. On a spiritual level, seek out a good book, teacher, or minister. The whole point is for you to recognize and accept where you are and then tend to the self in a holistic way.

We can learn a lot from weeds—is there an action, an emotion, a thought, or concept that is draining you? If you can recognize that this is a weed, that is sucking up more time and energy than it should, it may be helpful to picture it and go pull some weeds within your garden. See how easily they come up. If this energy is left unattended, it could end up taking over and consuming your life force—just pull it like you would a weed.

Our ancestors worked with plants on a medicinal level to heal the body, mind, and spirit. My ancestors, in particular, would harvest certain plants for washing their hair and bathing, to calm the mind and emotions, and to rebalance the spirit. As mentioned earlier when I shared how my ancestors learned to work with the peyote, the plant taught them. Other cultures may work with ayahuasca in order to become aware, heal, and grow. I am not recommending that you take part in one of these ceremonies—I am simply mentioning that this is another way that the plant kingdom can assist with health and well-being. However, if you do decide to take part in a healing ceremony of this nature, remember: each plant has a spirit and is alive, so honor it with this awareness. Additionally, do your research and find a trustworthy practitioner to take this journey with you.

Today, there are several examples of plants that we use for health and healing. We can work with aloe vera for skin inflammation. Mint is very beneficial when treating a cough or a cold. Lemongrass can assist with insomnia, stress, and general pain management. If these types of uses interest you, I would recommend learning more from a certified herbalist who can teach you what plants to use, how to prepare the plant for specific uses, and what the side effects might be. I am not an herbalist; however, I know many herbalists that I turn to for their knowledge and skill set.

Last, but certainly not least, have you ever heard of forest bathing? Take a walk in the forest and bathe in the sensation of the natural world. The body relaxes, your thoughts find peace, and you become calmer. You naturally heal. There are many sacred places within nature. The plant kingdom welcomes you home and can assist you with fresh air and a sense of oneness.

FOUR
Landscapes

My ancestors told me that the land carries spirits. That each landscape holds a different spirit—the spirits of the land. I'm sure that it is the same with many indigenous people and many spiritual belief systems as well. This is where we can start connecting and generating dialogue with the land itself. As stated earlier, all is energy and everything has a consciousness. This includes the land and the landscapes that we have here on Mother Earth. Earth is alive and holds many characteristics within the land itself. In the previous chapter we discussed how forests and plants communicate with each other; this is also the case with the land and its various environments that are expressed through landscapes.

I read a story once about the indigenous people of Australia. As they walked across the landscape they would tell a story, as though each landscape had its own story that must be shared. One day, an outsider wanted to hear the stories of the land. Unknowingly, the outsider invited the aboriginal individual to ride with him in his vehicle instead of walking across the land. The aboriginal agreed and jumped into the vehicle. The aboriginal had to talk and tell the story very, very quickly because of the vehicle's speed. As you could imagine, it was very difficult. Once understood, the outsider slowed the vehicle way down in order to hear the complete story of the land.[22] Pretty incredible!

So now, we have both the spirit of the land as well as individuals who will be able to translate the land's energy into a story. I have no doubt that the people who can tell the stories of the land are very mindful. Have you ever experienced this? Even to a small degree? An example of this could be taking a walk with someone who always says the same thing as they walk along a path. It is as if the land and the markers on the land are reminding that individual of a certain energy. When I was young my dad would drive us across the reservation, and at certain landmarks, he would always tell us the same story. It was like clockwork. Now I have a deeper understanding of why he may have done that.

If I were to show you a picture of my father and a picture of his birthplace, there would be many similarities. Nature has a funny way of taking on human characteristics. When I was a child I would see faces within the red rocks of the Navajo reservation.

One night I had a dream. In this dream, I saw the face of an old Indian man. His face was chiseled and his skin was ragged; the color was that of the earth. I was looking at his skin very closely as it was revealing itself to me. I began to zoom back to see a little bit bigger of a picture. I saw the palm of his hand with his fingers facing up. The hand's earth tone was old and ancient in color as well.

---

22. Abram, *Spell of the Sensuous*, 173.

I began to zoom back even farther in order to gain more insight as to what I was being shown. The farther back I went, the more I gained perspective. When I zoomed back far enough, I realized that I was actually looking at an old mountain.

Types of Landscapes

Landscapes can show us the environments that are present within any culture or subculture (including friends and family). We will be focusing on five major landscapes on the surface and / or biomes on Mother Earth: deserts, forests, mountains, grasslands, and jungles. Each of these holds a variety of plants and animals; however, the climates within these landscapes are varied, and this has an impact on what can grow and survive in each.

Deserts

The desert is a harsh place to live for most plants and animals due to its extreme temperatures and its virtually dry climate. Some deserts are so dry that rain has never been recorded to fall on them! Most deserts, if not all, appear to be flat. Deserts seem to encompass the extremities between hot and cold, life and death. During the day, the desert becomes very hot as the sun beats down. During the evening, the desert becomes very cold because there is no heat retention from the day.[23] The air is dry and so is the ground. The desert teaches us to conserve our resources, as this environment can be very limiting. Deserts appear to be barren and inhospitable, but for those species who can adapt to the desert, it can be a place of solitude.

---

23. Andrews, *Nature-Speak*, 198.

Forests

Forests hold a plethora of trees and plants. Forest covers about a third of the earth's surface. These trees can protect smaller wildlife from the sun, the rain, and the wind—an umbrella of sorts. Additionally, small animals can feed off the seeds that fall from the plants and trees.

Rain forests are very important because they assist with global weather patterns and rain. As the water evaporates from the rain forest, it can be carried to other areas, providing moisture. These environments are lush and moist year-round; hence, tropical natural life thrives in this environment. The rain forest shows us how to grow free of controls and constriction. However, this causes the trees to have thinner bark, as thick bark is not necessary to protect the trees from colder weather. Therefore, only thin-skinned trees can thrive here.

Did you know that tropical rain forests are home to almost half of all the animal species on earth?[24] Many rain forests contain lifeforms that we still haven't discovered; hence, it is an environment of mystery.[25]

Mountains

Mountains are Mother Earth's giants. They are powerful and stand strong. Mountains cover about a fourth of the earth's surface. For the most part, they are higher in altitude. Generally, as altitude increases, the temperature gets cooler, yet the sun is more intense. There is a vast fluctuation in temperature, sometimes within one day. My husband and I took a road trip to Mount Evans in Colorado

24. Nunez, "Rainforests, Explained."

25. Andrews, *Nature-Speak*, 202.

a few years back. When we started at the bottom of the mountain, the ambient temperature was about eighty degrees Fahrenheit. It took us about thirty minutes to travel to the top of the mountain, where we found snow! The ambient temperature was below freezing. Within thirty minutes, we experienced a fifty-degree temperature fluctuation due to the change in elevation. And yes, when we got down the mountain, it was still eighty degrees out.

Mountains provide a challenge to be climbed and may provide a little seclusion for anyone that is looking for it. Mountains may provide more than seclusion—there are many legends about meeting great spirits at the top of a mountain.

Grasslands

Grasslands are vast areas of open field and cover more than a fifth of the earth's surface. These large fields of tall grass have hardly any trees. They are one of Mother Earth's most productive landscapes: the grasslands support and sustain many populations of large animal herds, such as elephants, bison, zebras, and lions. However, because of this, there is a lot of competition in this environment, especially between predators. The grasslands provide us with plenty of room to grow and sustain.

Jungles

And finally, look toward the jungle. The jungle is full of trees and wildlife; however, the jungle can also be somewhat dangerous. Within a jungle, you will find a lot of intense competition and struggle to survive. Jungles are like thick tropical forests with a high level of humidity, dense vegetation, and a plethora of trees. Although the jungle is much like the rain forest, I included it as its own category because it indicates a less organized environment.

In literature, the word "jungle" often indicates a primitive, wild, untamed place: "It's a jungle out there!" "Eat or be eaten!"

Again, when we are learning from the natural world and looking at our lives through the lenses of the landscape that nature reveals, we are looking at the environment—or culture and subculture—within each situation. Yes, we can align ourselves and our personalities with how we interact and what we look for in the animal kingdom and the plant kingdom; however, landscapes reveal the atmosphere of the situation.

Relationships & Romance

As we discussed earlier, relationships are like a dance. The landscape would be like the dance floor. When we look at the landscape or the environment of a relationship, there are many things that dictate this. What dictates a culture or subculture? Take a moment and think about your answer. I will offer up some of my ideas; however, I would encourage you to come up with some of your own as well.

There are many things that will influence a culture: where someone grew up, their age or the time frame they grew up in, and the way that they communicate with each other, to name a few. Each culture has its own norms and patterns that they have always done. When you are looking at a relationship, you must examine each individual first; what type of culture did they grow up in? This will allow you to understand individuals' norms and reality.

When two people are getting to know each other, they ask each other common questions: *What music do you like? Where did you grow up? How old are you?* I believe that people do this in order to understand where realities are shared and where they are not. What are the ties that bind people together so that we can understand each other? Everyday questions will also help you understand what type of family the individual grew up in. Was it a large family with important traditions and big dinners? This helps you understand the type of environment that seems normal to this individual. Do they come from a small family? Are they an only child? I'm not a psychologist or sociologist, so I will not attempt to draw assumptions about large families or single-child families and how they affect a person's psychology; however, these are the beginnings of getting to know the other person's norms and realities in order to better understand the individual.

Additionally, it is good to ask yourself these questions so that you understand what your own norms and realities are. Once you do this, you have the ability to understand yourself and the other person, which will help you see what atmosphere the two of you naturally create together.

A relationship's environment or landscape can also be influenced by finances, how close or far people live from each other, and how much available time they have to spend together. These things certainly can impact the landscape within a relationship. Let's look at the various landscapes that nature reveals to us and discuss what can live in each of these environments.

Earlier the desert was described as harsh, dry, and barren, with extreme temperatures. It offers solitude. This may describe your relationship. Maybe your wife or husband is overseas, so the ground is dry and there is a lot of solitude. Maybe you're in a relationship that is very passionate and the chemistry feels hot, much like the sun beating on the ground, but it can grow cold quickly. The extremes in temperature could feel like the relationship is all or nothing; there is an uneven push and pull. Maybe you're in a relationship that seems flat.

If you are like a snake or a lizard, the desert is your preferred landscape. But if you are like a tropical bird or fish, this environment will not work for you. If you relate yourself to a cactus or a small shrub, you can certainly survive in this landscape. However, if you are like many plants, you will dry up in this relationship. What other ideas can you think of? Again, none of this is good or bad. None of this is right or wrong. It is what it is, and that is what nature shows us. The question is, does it work for you?

Earlier we described the forest as a plethora of growth, a place to grow and create without controls or constrictions. Forests are also somewhat mysterious. Tall trees protect the ground from the sun, rain, and wind. This allows room for new growth to spring up and thrive. If you are in a relationship that is like the forest, this relationship allows you to be creative. It also provides you with an unrestricted landscape to grow your new ideas. Maybe you have a lot of little ideas that you would like to grow—some of which may become trees. This relationship allows you to do so! As lovely as this sounds, not all individuals are comfortable in this type of relationship. If you relate to a cactus, this environment would make you very uncomfortable because of all the moisture (or emotion). Maybe you enjoy your solitude and this environment is too much for you, or maybe you like a little bit more of a challenge within a relationship ... which brings us to the mountains.

We describe the mountains as a challenge that provides an opportunity to grow. The mountains are strong and powerful. There are many stories about an individual going on a journey, climbing a mountain, and returning home a changed person. Maybe this is the adventure for you! Relationships that are like mountains require people to grow in and through the relationship, and the relationship often lasts for decades. Maybe mountain relationships have the ability to endure life's challenges. Through the relationship, each individual navigates the highs and lows—the peaks and valleys. And, because of their relationship, the couple may believe a legend of their own. I think that people in the public eye often have these types of relationships.

When looking at the mountains, altitude is in play here as well. As we go up in altitude, the air becomes thinner and the sun is a little more intense. We need to slowly ascend the mountain in order to acclimate and reacclimate to the environment. Hence, if a relationship is the landscape of the mountain, you may want to take it slow. See the challenges ahead of you; do not hide from them, but prepare for them. Rise to the challenge and grow tall, strong, and powerful!

Now let's examine the grasslands. Earlier we described the grasslands as the environment that has plenty of room to grow. We also described it as having the most populations of large animal herds. We looked at competition in numbers and also in predators. It's funny because the comparison that came to my mind was internet dating. Be careful out there, and rely on your herd. Maybe the grassland is suggesting you have a great group of friends or colleagues, and/or maybe you're simply dating a lot of people. This could indicate an open relationship as well. It is good to note that some relationships move through different landscapes, meaning that relationships can change over time, and what is required of the relationship may change as well.

Earlier we described the jungle as being wild, untamed, and primitive. There is intense competition and a struggle to survive. It is also dangerous. If you find yourself in this type of relationship setting, you must be very agile and alert. This could indicate a one-night stand or friends with benefits. Make sure that you are up for the challenge and have the ability to turn on a dime. What pops into my mind is the local bar or nightclub. Maybe this landscape is right for you at this time in your life—perhaps you want to sow your wild oats, so to speak. Again, the jungle landscape is not right or wrong. Jungles are not good or bad. Jungles are simply jungles—wild.

At this point, I would invite you to remember what type of animal you relate to the most. What environment or landscape does that animal thrive in? Also consider what plant you identified with the most. What environment does that plant thrive in? I encourage you to define the landscape that allows you to grow into your own authenticity in all of your relationships.

Business & Finance

Now we get to apply the natural world's teachings of landscapes within business and finance. It is good to consider that different industries will be more successful in one landscape than another. It is also good to consider that some landscapes may be less conducive to growth. Think about your financial situation and what environment will increase your return on investment (ROI). Since we are talking about the landscape being like the environment, please feel free to draw on correlations within the economy. And as we shift gears from relationships to business, please consider the relationships and the connections that you make in your career.

The desert is a harsh, dry environment. The desert teaches us to conserve our resources, as they may be limited. From an economic standpoint, this sounds like the Great Depression, a time of limited resources. If the economy is behaving like the desert, you must make career choices that are conducive to this dry environment. If your finances move into the landscape of the desert, it may be time to look for external assistance. The key here is that you recognize that you are in a desert and use your resources. Many say that you should save for a rainy day—I say that you should save for time in the desert!

There are some industries or fields of work that can survive in the desert. Think about the fact that deserts may not get rain for one hundred days, but then one day the rain comes in and it is a downpour. This relates to people who have one or two big influxes of money a couple of times a year. These survivors may enjoy this type of environment.

Now let's look through the lenses of the landscape of the forest as we consider the economy, careers, and finances. The forest has a plethora of growth. From an economic standpoint, this feels like a bull market. Additionally, the forest has an umbrella of tall trees to protect the ground from too much sun, rain, or wind; it keeps the ground moist. This is a good environment for mom and pop shops, which may be funded by an investor umbrella, and entrepreneurs. This is the time to invest and to grow your financial situation. This is a time to start something new within your field or industry—this landscape is extremely conducive to growth.

Mountains can be the symbol of starting out on a long journey and growing through the challenges, through the highs and lows, in a slower and more grounded manner. Economically, I would consider the Industrial Revolution and how that changed the playing field. I would also look at computers and how they have changed the world. Regarding careers, mountains remind me of big business. I would look at the top one hundred or top five hundred companies. This landscape is conducive to taking a journey—starting at the bottom and working your way to the top, literally. This indicates a time of slowly growing your career and/or reputation; give it the time that it needs. When thinking of the mountain landscape in regard to finances, I think of a mountain of money, which could also indicate an inheritance or bonus.

Now let's move over to the grasslands and look at how that environment relates to finance. Earlier, the grasslands were described as a place of competition in numbers. They are also a place where there is plenty of room to grow and sustain. Grasslands have many populations of large herds. From an economic position, I would say that the grasslands are like big industries—healthcare, technology, construction, retail, etc. There are many companies within these fields, much like a herd of animals working together. These settings may be very competitive. However, there are plenty of opportunities. Unlike the forest environment, the grasslands are conducive to joining a larger group instead of starting up your own thing. From a financial point of view, I would recommend pooling money in order to achieve growth in the stock market.

Last, but certainly not least, the jungle. The jungle is described as wild, untamed, and primitive, with intense competition. From an economic position, this would indicate an environment of big swings to the right or left. I think about the vines in the jungle and how monkeys use them to travel, swinging from one vine to the next. Career-wise, it makes me think of becoming a rock star and/or movie star. One day you could be part of the commonfolk, and the next day you could get discovered. The jungle relates to a career path that can be wild and untamed with a lot of competition. Maybe you're up for that and maybe you're not; it is all up to you and what you feel comfortable with and/or what type of challenges you like. With regard to finances, the jungle is a high-risk environment. If you are going to invest, make sure that you can also afford to lose the investment. That is not to say that you will lose your investment; it is simply risky. One can also make a lot of money from high-risk environments. Just be aware.

Health & Well-Being

Now, we can examine landscapes in regard to health and well-being. First, let's reflect on the four bodies that have existence, outlined in the introduction: the physical body, emotional body, mental body, and spiritual body. Next, add the understanding that your landscape is the environment in which you exist. Reflect on the idea that each body can be in the same environment at the same time and/or different environments at the same time. Yes, humans can be very complex at times. With this in mind, let's proceed.

If the physical body is in the desert, this would be literal. Maybe you live in Arizona or New Mexico. Whether or not you like it there is up to you. However, if your emotional body is in the desert, this could indicate solitude, having a dry sense of humor, or feeling harsh. Potentially, you may have come out of a relationship and you wish to be alone for a while. Maybe you're going through a dry spell emotionally. If your mental body is in the desert, this could indicate the need for a refreshing thought or idea, or you may need a little break from everybody else. If you are spiritually in the desert, maybe this is a time of purification—you're working through some things. Or maybe you just don't feel inspired at this time. Apply it however you wish. Allow the desert to speak to you.

If the physical body is in the forest, it is literal. Maybe you live amongst a lot of trees or are in a place where your physical body feels safe. If your emotional body is in the forest, this is a time to express yourself, because you are protected. If your mental body is in the forest, this is a wonderful time to journal, write, or create a new idea, as it will thrive. If your spiritual body is in the forest, this could be an indication of more spiritual growth, yet you feel grounded and are moving into the great mystery.

If your physical body is in the landscape of the mountains, again this could be literal. Perhaps you are getting exercise and challenging yourself to become stronger. If your emotional body is within the mountainous landscape, you are growing and maturing emotionally by feeling the peaks and valleys. If your mental body is in the mountains, you may be learning a new concept and "going back to school," so to speak—anything that challenges your mind to grow. And finally, if your spiritual body is in the mountains, as the legends say, your spirit is on a journey, climbing higher and higher through the challenges in order to meet the great spirit. You will come back changed.

If your physical body is in the grasslands, you most likely live in a situation with wide-open spaces and room to run free. If your emotional body is in the grasslands, this could reveal a desire to be a part of a group: you may want to feel that emotional support that a herd provides. If your mental body is in the grasslands, you may think about life in terms of playing chess—i.e., you are very strategic—or maybe you enjoy being a part of the think tank and thinking with others. If your spiritual body is in the grasslands, you enjoy being around people who have the same beliefs as you. It could also show that you recognize that you are free to grow and sustain in many directions.

If your physical body is in the jungle, this indicates that you are physically living in a place that may seem wild and/or untamed. Maybe you are struggling to survive and need to stay alert. If you find your emotional body to be in the jungle, you have a wild heart and move through life in a nontraditional way. However, if your mental body is in the jungle, your mind thinks about intense competition and/or you have a more primitive or primal type of thought process. You may think that we live in a "dog-eat-dog world." If your spiritual body is in the jungle, you may be wild and outside the box.

There are many more landscapes in our world. Is there a landscape that you want to focus on to extract its wisdom? I wanted to offer you the ability to connect with landscapes—whatever a landscape says to you is perfect and pure. A landscape changes and morphs; may this provide you with the inspiration to make it your own.

FIVE
The Seasons and Weather Cycles

The seasons within the natural world are defined as spring, summer, autumn, and winter. Each of these seasons is overarching and may impact where we go, what we wear, and even what we eat. So it is within the seasons of our lives. At times we are in a season of newness like the spring. Sometimes we are in a growth period, much like the summertime. Maybe it is time to reap the rewards of something you have accomplished; this is like the autumn's harvest. And there are the times when we feel like spending a little time alone, hibernating like a bear would in the winter.

The Seasons

Seasons continue to flow in a cycle when naturally moving forward. The ancestors tell us that our lives flow through seasons just like the natural world does. The difference is that each season within our lives is not subject to a three-month period of time. We can move through a season in as little as a few weeks, or it may take years. When we are aware of what season we are in within our lives, then we can honor that season and navigate accordingly. If we resist the season that we're in, it will cause stagnancy within ourselves. When we become stagnant, we are not growing and/or moving—we are fixed within that season for an extended amount of time. Embrace what season you are in and continue to flow through your seasons naturally and organically.

In this chapter we will discuss the seasons of the year and what they bring into our lives, how the weather within each season can impact us both physically and metaphorically, the changes within these seasons, and how to work with these concepts in order to better understand our lives, relationships, finances, and health. Let's begin by looking at the four main seasons—spring, summer, autumn, and winter.

Spring

In the spring, the weather begins to warm up and the days become longer. As the snow turns into rain, the ground begins to soften beneath our feet. Flowers begin to grow, and the grass once again turns green. The trees that once were dormant begin to wake up as the roots return sap to the branches. The spring's burgeoning brings new life. Springtime is a time to sow seeds and plant a garden—to start something new or to renew something old. What will you grow?

Summer

When it is summertime, the heat of the sun changes the weather even more—summer is very warm, even hot. This season can draw us outside to play and have adventures. Friends and families get together for picnics and barbecues; it is a very sociable time. There are warm breezes and life is abounding. Summer is a time of gaining, growing, and social pursuits. You begin to grow what you have planted in the spring—be mindful.

Autumn

During autumn the weather begins to cool down. The days become shorter and the nights become longer. Fresh smells of harvest are in the air. Leaves begin to change color and release from the branches. Trees begin to fall back to sleep as sap returns to the root system within Mother Earth. This is a time to wrap up outside projects and consider moving events indoors for the winter.

Winter

In the winter, the weather becomes cold and icy in many climates. Snow falls upon the ground like a blanket to put Mother Earth to sleep again for a season. The days become shorter and the nights become longer. Even if you do not live in an area that experiences snow and cold, the metaphor here is the main takeaway. Winter is a time to go within; hibernate if necessary.

People roll through seasons much like Mother Earth rolls through seasons, except that our seasons are not limited to a specific metered time; they ebb and flow as we roll through them. Some personal seasons can last a few days or a few years. Take note of what season you are in and make it the best possible. Nature does not complain about the winter and the cold; it just is. Nature does not complain about a hot summer day; it just is. Natural law accepts opposites, even extreme opposites. Yes, we may prefer one season over another; however, in order to appreciate the whole, we must experience and accept the whole.

Equinox and Solstice

Here we are going to examine the equinoxes and solstices. The vernal equinox announces spring around March 21 (or when the sun enters zero degrees Aries). The summer solstice announces summer around June 21 (or when the sun enters zero degrees Cancer). The autumnal equinox announces autumn right around September 21 (or when the sun enters zero degrees Libra). Finally, the winter solstice announces winter around December 21 (or when the sun enters zero degrees Capricorn). These dates may vary a little from year to year.

Although there is a specific calendar day for each of these changes, it still is not a clear, clean break within the weather cycles. The weather cycles will overlap and alternate between the seasons. So it is within our lives as we move through these seasons and weather cycles. At times it may feel like the environment of your relationship, career, or health might be warming up; we still might experience a little coldness before the environment completely shifts from one season to another. Please do not get discouraged when this happens—it is a natural flow of shifting.

Equinox

An equinox is when both hemispheres are experiencing equal sunlight; twelve hours of day and twelve hours of night. If we were to personalize this concept that Mother Earth shows us, we could say that this is the perfect balance between the yin and the yang energies within us. Twelve hours of day could be interpreted as twelve hours of yang, and the twelve hours of night would then represent the yin energy.

As day turns to night and night to day, there is a twilight period that we move through. At this time there is an anticipation of the sun rising or of nightfall. We experience this effect all over the globe. But what is this twilight teaching us? Have you ever had the feeling that something was going to happen, but you couldn't put your finger on what it was or how you knew? At times a change can be felt before it occurs, whether you are anticipating something wonderful or dreadful. This would be a twilight period within our life. Twilight time can teach us how to feel the current energy, sense that a change is coming, and prepare for this change. How can you prepare for something that you cannot put your finger on? Let your body teach you.

Your body can sense when nightfall is coming. Maybe you start your evening routine by shutting off the lights, closing the windows, or relaxing with a good book. In one way or another, you begin to settle in—settle into your homes and settle into yourself. Unless, of course, you are a night owl or work at night, in which case your body begins to prepare for work or enjoyment; there is an anticipation of getting ready and becoming more alert. This is the same sensation that many individuals will feel in the morning, getting up and getting ready for a day of activity. Either way, this is twilight energy in effect within our lives.

To be clear, although the actual twilight happens in the morning and evening of every day, this does not limit the twilight energy in our lives and in our individual stories. Twilight energy can last for days, weeks, and even months. It is that feeling that something is about to occur and/or change. Many individuals find themselves excited, afraid, or confused during this period. If you are in one of these periods, spend time in the actual twilight and feel the natural support of what is occurring.

Solstice

The summer solstice and winter solstice have their similarities and differences. The summer solstice marks the longest day and the shortest night; the winter solstice marks the longest night and the shortest day. So, if yang energy is daytime energy, one could correlate the summer solstice with yang and the domination of this energy. Yang energy is described as masculine and bright. The winter solstice would be yin energy. Yin energy is described as feminine and dark. The balance between the two energies is displayed in the time of the equinoxes, and the domination of one energy over the other would be revealed within the solstices.

Nature is showing us that there is time for equilibrium within these energies and that there is dominance between the two. However, if there is a dominance of one over the other, there will come a time when the pendulum swings the other way in order to rebalance these energies. This is a wonderful teaching of the seasons: nature continues to balance and rebalance itself. Although there may be a huge swing one way, nature shows us that a huge swing in the other direction is coming in time.

Relationships & Romance

The concept here with relationships and romance is to recognize that you may be in one season within the relationship and the other person may be in a different season than you. Moreover, the relationship may be in a season of its own. With this in mind, consider what season you are in within the relationship; note that this may be a different season than where you are personally. To clarify this thought, please allow me to provide an example of what I am attempting to say.

Let's say that I am experiencing summertime within my personal life—I am gaining and growing and may want to be creative and connect with other people. However, what if I am in winter within my relationship, meaning that my relationship feels cold? Additionally, let's say that my partner is also in the summertime of their life and the wintertime of our relationship. This means that we are gaining and growing outside of the relationship and the relationship is quiet and still; this may be comfortable and welcoming, or it might not be. Finally, the relationship may be in a season all its own. Maybe the relationship is in autumn; this could indicate a time within the relationship when we are letting go of old definitions of our relationship, or maybe we are letting go of the relationship altogether.

✦✦✦ EXERCISE 8 ✦✦✦
Relationship

There are many different combinations of relationships and seasons, so here is a list of the five things to keep in mind when applying this concept:

1. What season am I in, personally?
2. What season is the other person experiencing?
3. What season am I experiencing in my relationship?
4. What season is the other person experiencing in the relationship?
5. What season is our relationship in?

This exercise can shed a lot of light on a relationship, whether it is with friends, family, or a romantic
partner. Remember, we all roll through seasons, individually and within our relationships.

Let's look at some examples to open up this concept more.

Every relationship is a dance, and all relationships roll through
seasons. Each season brings its own vibration and has conversations with other seasons from its positioning and understanding of
the other season. Some people are most comfortable within one
season; they don't appreciate other seasons. First, think about what
season you most enjoy and what seasons are more difficult for you.
Next, understand that everybody has their own preference for a
variety of reasons. Finally, begin to understand your own unique
perception of each season while understanding that other people
may perceive the world totally differently—and at times, totally
opposite of you.

If I am personally in springtime, I am looking at the world
around me as fresh, new, and coming to life. I am planting seeds
and gaining and growing. If I then run across someone who is in
summertime, I may be encouraged by their progress and want to
learn from this person, as they are revealing to me what is to come.
However, if I meet someone who is in autumn, I might find that
everything moves through cycles; it could provide insight into what
I am planting now and what it will harvest into later. And if I meet
someone who is in the winter, I may feel like encouraging them,
reminding them that soon the spring will come. You can add your
own verbiage here depending on how you view the seasons. Also,
recognize that this will be true of the other people who are in a
relationship with you—it goes both ways. They may be experienc-

ing spring, and depending on where you are and how they view that season, they will act accordingly to you. This paragraph covers question one and question two of the exercise—what season you are in, personally, and what season the other person is in.

Now let's reflect on question three and question four—what season are you in within the relationship, and what season is the other person in within the relationship? Again, remember that some people are more comfortable in one season than another. This would be a great conversation to have with anyone that you are in a relationship with (unless they are not open to it, in which case they may think you are crazy and wonder where you got all these ideas; if you find yourself in this situation, feel free to blame Granddaughter Crow).

If the relationship makes you feel like you are supported and ready to start a new project, this indicates that the relationship is warm enough for you to grow. If the relationship makes you feel like you can be footloose and fancy-free, this means that the relationship causes you to feel as though you are in the summer. If the relationship causes you to look at how far you've come and to reap the rewards of everything that you have done, and/or if it feels more karmic or like a lesson is to be learned within the relationship, this could very well indicate that the relationship places you in the season of autumn. It is good to note here that autumn doesn't mean that the relationship is over, although at times relationships that are coming to a close will be in the autumn; it is simply a matter of where you are and what you are looking for. If the relationship causes you to do some deep inner reflection, this could indicate winter. Also, it is good to note that some individuals like the winter and some do not, so some people feel comfortable if the relationship causes them to feel a little cold, and some will seek to exit the relationship because they can't stand the coldness.

Finally, let us approach question five—what season is the relationship itself in, as its own entity? If the relationship is in the spring, the relationship is growing in new directions. If the relationship is in the summer, there is a lot of light and clarity within the relationship. If the relationship is in autumn, you are reaping the rewards of what you have grown within the relationship and deciding what you will or will not plant next spring. If the relationship is in the winter, this is a relationship of fewer words and more space; if you like the winter, for you it may be a time of hibernation together. Either option is valid, depending on your perception of the season.

Remember, it is natural to roll through different seasons within a relationship; relationships can be so complex and dynamic. The art is to be aware and to learn from the seasons. Apply the concepts that the seasons have brought to us. Additionally, recognize how you approach each season—each season may speak differently to you. This is key to recognizing your relationships' seasons, as seasons don't speak in words; they speak in the phenomenon.

At times you will have sunny days; other times a little rain will fall. Each season will come with its own set of weather patterns.

Business & Finance

The application of seasons to business and finance is something that is not so far-fetched. There are a handful of sayings that do this for us. For example, "make hay while the sun shines," which means to do all that you can in business because the economy is good. Additionally, "saving up for a rainy day," which means setting aside some finances just in case you get hit with something unexpected. The correlation between business/finance and seasons/weather may seem a little more natural.

✦✦✦ **EXERCISE 9** ✦✦✦
Career

There are a variety of applications of the seasons within your career. One application would be to first view what season you are personally in within your career. Are you just starting out in your field? If so, this would simulate springtime. Spring is a time to plant seeds and to gain and grow. Maybe you have been in your career for a little while and you're looking for more growth; this would indicate summertime, a time of social invitations and creative pursuits. Maybe it is time to connect with others within your industry to see what other opportunities there are available for you. Maybe you are very seasoned within your career and have a solid reputation; this would be indicative of autumn. It is time to reap the rewards of everything that you have done and the rewards of your solid reputation. This is a time when you may have many opportunities knocking at your door, or maybe you can do your work with your eyes closed, so to speak. Are you a little bored? Are you considering retirement? This could indicate wintertime within your personal career. Many of us change career paths within our lifetime; maybe you are older but in the springtime of a new industry. There are many applications that can be thought of; I invite you to come up with some of your own. Feel free to be creative, and allow the seasons to speak to you.

Next, look at the season that each industry is in. Is it a new up-and-coming industry (spring) or an old industry that is going to become irrelevant (winter)? Maybe the industry that you are looking at is a very sociable industry with a lot of creative pursuits and plenty of room to grow—this would indicate an industry that is in the summertime, or a summertime industry. Or maybe the industry that you are looking at has reaped many rewards and has a seasoned reputation; this could be an industry that is in the autumn, or an autumn industry. With these thoughts in mind, align yourself with the industry that best suits you. As you would imagine, industries roll through their own seasons as well.

Some industries will have the characteristics of one particular season. For example, I would say that technology companies tend to waver between spring, the season of new ideas, and the summer, expanding upon these new ideas. I think that some technology, such as phones and computers, tends to be outdated as quickly as it comes on the market. This is a fast-moving industry, whereas oil and gas companies tend to behave more like dinosaurs: they're old, large, and have their own culture. If you work with an older company, you could bring some new ideas with you. This would be an example of an individual who is in the springtime of their career going into the wintertime of an industry. Think of the metaphors that would surround this example. You would have to be a warm spring to melt some of the snow of the winter company. It would be a challenge, but maybe you're up for it.

There is also a literal interpretation here. Some industries actually do better in the spring; others do better in another season. For example, the clothing industry changes with the seasons. Holidays impact a lot of sales within certain industries. So if you are in one of these fields, I encourage you to capitalize on each season and each holiday. Then again, you probably already know this. So maybe I'm speaking to an entrepreneur, inviting them to pay attention to the seasons and how they can capitalize on each one.

Now let's look at our financial state through the lenses of the seasons. One would easily understand if I said that my bank account was cold, or that it's a rainy day for me, or even that my portfolio is gaining. As stated earlier, we often utilize the metaphor of seasons and/or weather patterns when speaking about financial situations. I will not bore you with the application of each of the seasons and your personal finances because I'm sure you understand. However, what I would like to do is to introduce the concept of planning ahead. Everything flows in cycles and everything rolls through seasons; this includes your financial position. Hence, it would serve you well to rejoice in the spring, when you are investing your finances, and to be thankful in the summer as your portfolio gains and grows. Reap the rewards of autumn, yet tuck some away for winter so that you have some finances to plant again in the spring.

When I was in my twenties, I was managing little shops or apartment complexes—locally owned businesses. Out of the blue, I was blessed with an opportunity to work for an international company. I had a small family at the time, and we needed to secure and stabilize our home. So obviously, I jumped on this opportunity. However, I was in the springtime when it came to corporate America, let alone an international company. I had a massive learning curve. At times the stress would hit me so hard that I would find myself in tears when I got home from work. My tears behaved like the rain of spring, as the next day I would get up, put a smile on my face, and get back to work. It took me about six months to completely feel comfortable in my new environment. But I gained and grew from the experience, and soon I mastered the position and was handed a promotion.

For the next twelve years, I went through cycles within my career. At times I was asked to learn things—spring. I was asked to connect with our investors and to go to conferences—summer. I received a bonus or recognition—autumn. And after twelve years, I definitely found myself in the winter. I began to feel cold and hard (or simply businesslike, in my industry). I began to feel like I was turning into someone that I was not. Instead of staying in that cold environment and freezing up inside, I decided to open up my own company—Major Consulting, LLC. Spring is here again!

Or so I thought. Although I could equate starting your own company as springtime—you are planting seeds, getting your name out there, etc.—where I found myself was in an economic winter: the recession of 2008. At that time, most people and companies were cutting or trimming their budgets. Unfortunately, I was planting my seeds in the winter; this is not the best time to expect growth. So I took another job with the state government and ran my business part-time.

The funny thing about government entities is that they are much like dinosaurs. As I was working for a branch of the government, they were "reorganizing." That is exactly what management continued to say; they would not give details, and maybe they did not have them. But there is only so long that you can leave a large group of people in the dark before those people start to turn into a group that has a low tolerance for being in an ambiguous state. So, the leadership team made a few choices and a few cuts. The employees assumed that it was all over and they could settle in and get back to work.

However, the leadership team was not done with that "reorganization." Employees caught wind that there was still reorganizing going on. As you would expect, people began to fear for their jobs. This is scary, but it's even scarier during a recession. This went back and forth for a good year. The tension in Cubicleville was high!

One day, one of the executives called me into her office. She asked me what the pulse of the employees was at that time. I told her that it was tense.

She said, "Why? The reorganization project is over. Why aren't they happy that they still have their jobs?"

She did not understand, so I looked at her and said, "Why are you surprised that it is snowing in the winter?"

I share this story with you to provide you with an example that some of you can probably relate to. There are many examples to draw from. What is your career story in relation to the seasons and weather patterns?

Health & Well-Being

I really enjoy working with the four bodies of existence—physical, emotional, mental, and spiritual. In this section, we will begin to apply the wisdom of the seasons to the four bodies of existence. Here we go ...

Spring

Spring is a time of planting seeds. On a physical level, you can plant literal seeds and grow fruits, nuts, berries, or vegetables. On a metaphoric level, you can work with the energy of the spring to grow anything on the physical plane. For example, the burgeoning of spring holds the energy of things coming to life or returning to life once again. Therefore, you may want to take some time in the spring to sit under a tree and mindfully observe with all of your five senses. Write or talk about what springtime phenomena draws up within you. Apply it to a project that you've been wanting to start. Plant those seeds in the spring.

On an emotional level, what seeds do you want to plant? Under that tree, get in touch with your heart. Would you like to feel more peace, gratitude, or self-love? Take a moment and begin to consider the various ideas that come; this can increase these sensations within your emotional body. One idea is to meditate more. Another idea is to start a gratitude list and see what you are truly grateful for within your life. Maybe you decide to get a massage or buy yourself something that you've had your eye on. Those are a few quick thoughts—take time to come up with ideas that fit your lifestyle. The energy of spring can teach you how to do this, and it can show you how to begin implementing these ideas in your life.

On a mental level, spring teaches us that we can create new ideas and adapt new approaches to current situations. When I fall into a mental rut, I do my best to look at the world from a different perspective. Sometimes I do this literally. Trying driving a different way to the store, or brush your teeth with your nondominant hand. This creates new thought patterns by developing new neural pathways, allowing you to think in a different way. Mentally, you can sow new ideas that will grow into something wonderful; stimulate the mind to think in different ways. Food for thought.

On a spiritual level, work with the energy of spring to start a new routine, or to add an additional practice to your routine, in order to grow spiritually. Take a class, read a book, or take a walk and journal. Plant some new ideas or listen to another concept. It takes a strong mind to entertain an idea that it decides not to adopt. I say this because people get to entertain all sorts of ideas and decide if they wish to adopt them or not. There are endless ways to grow spiritually and to connect with self—and that which is outside self.

Summer

Summertime is here—this is the time to grow and socialize. On a physical level, summertime will literally grow grass and the plants in the garden that you started in the spring. However, it doesn't end there—apply the teachings of summertime to anything in your physical existence. Again, go back to that tree and experience your surroundings with all of your five senses. Next, journal and/ or chat about the phenomenon with a friend—or with the tree itself! Return to the list of projects that you may have written in the spring and tend to them. Shine more light on them to help them grow. Tend to it, shed light on it, water it, and it will grow. These are the teachings of the summertime.

On an emotional level, continue to grow those lovely experiences that you planted in the spring. Are you still meditating? It is all up to you. If you stopped meditating, call it a pause and start it up again. There is no shame in this, as far as I am concerned. Emotionally, this may be a time of social engagements and connecting with others. Nurture these relationships through action and outdoor activities. I love the summertime—it makes me feel so connected to the world around me and to others. There are so many ways to continue to grow; this is the teaching of summertime.

On a mental level, this is a beautiful time to engage, develop, and allow for more clarity and ideas to grow. Keep reading those books and talking to others about inspirational or deep concepts. Keep those conversations going and growing. Summer is the time to grow ideas and new mental pathways. Since summertime draws us outside, metaphorically, on a mental level, this could mean to think outside the box. Mentally, take new ideas and develop them to prepare for the autumn harvest.

✦✦✦ EXERCISE 10 ✦✦✦
Be a Tree

On a spiritual level, summertime is about active growth. I defer to the tree to share its summertime lessons.

I invite you to take a moment and breathe. Gently close your eyes and visualize that you are a tree. Allow your energy to move from your feet downward into Mother Earth, like the roots of the tree. Feel her nourishment and draw that energy up.

Allow this energy to move up through your body and stretch your arms to the heavens, like the branches of a tree. Visualize your branches growing up toward the sky, above the clouds, and high into the heavens, where there is a light source. Touch that light source and allow it to flow down through you, through your body, and back to Mother Earth.

Keep doing this until you wish to stop. Gently open your eyes and feel what you feel.

After completing that exercise, I feel grounded, centered, and aware. Summertime is a time of clarity, with the bright sunshine bringing light to any darkness.

Autumn

Autumn, a time of harvest. On a physical level, autumn is a time to reap the rewards of the harvest. You can literally harvest the plants from your garden. Wouldn't it be fun to return to the same tree you visited during springtime and to note all of the differences that have taken place between spring and autumn? Look at how far you have come and the adventures that you have had along the way. Feel this season with your five senses—what is the next step in each of your projects? Maybe it is time to let go of one or to hand one off to the next person, Maybe it is time to celebrate, as the project is done. Allow autumn to teach you.

On an emotional level, allow autumn to cool you down into a calming period. This is a wonderful time to reflect. Were you able to experience peace, gratitude, and/or self-love? What goals did you set for yourself in the spring? What seeds did these goals plant? Do you feel more like yourself now? When you allow yourself to experience peace, or any other emotion you want to, it is amazing. Celebrate the harvest of your emotional growth and development that spring and summer walked you through.

Mentally, you are now able to harvest the manifestation of the idea that you planted in the spring and grew in the summer. On a mental level, autumn demonstrates how to gently let go of old ideas, like the leaves on the tree that gently release and dance down the street. Allow your active mind to rest and let go. Don't be concerned—next spring will bring more ideas. Autumn teaches us that letting go of the old is natural.

On a spiritual level, autumn is a time of recognition and realization. Think about how much you have grown and the benefits of the growth you just experienced. It is a wonderful time to reflect on how far you have come. Life isn't always easy—nature teaches us this—but life encourages us to grow, and if we are paying attention, we will grow. Take time to reflect on how far you have come—pat yourself on the back and breathe. Congratulations!

Winter

Winter has come—a time to go within and review the year. Physically, people are drawn indoors where it is warmer; the days become shorter and the nights become longer. You are able to eat the fruit of your labor throughout the past three seasons. This is also a wonderful time to keep your friends and family close; feel the warmth of celebration and appreciation. Enjoy the feeling of home. This may be the time to take the projects that you've been working on and internalize them, or bring them closer to you and keep them warm.

On an emotional level, winter probably causes you to withdraw a little more. Emotionally, this is the time when you can experience a deeper connection with the intimate relationships in your life. At times, you even may want to isolate for a bit—winter teaches us how to do this and shows us that it is natural. Pay attention to the desires of your heart so that you know what you would like to plant next spring.

On a mental level, winter is a good time to be at peace and to reflect even more. Mentally, this is a time to take stock of your thoughts and to release the ones that are no longer working for you. It is a time to go deeper—pay attention to any and all thoughts. Thoughts are things. From thoughts, actions come. From action, you manifest your world. Pay attention to your thoughts and continue to be mindful.

On a spiritual level, winter is a time of rest and revival. Spiritually, it is a time of deeper and more meaningful connection. It is a time to go within, self-reflect, and meditate (although I do recommend reflecting and meditating during every season). Winter is the time to slow down and take notice of what is within. Be strong and know what you know.

Here's the kicker: the four main seasons will teach us the cycle of the natural world, but you might not be in the same emotional, mental, or spiritual season as the physical season. Maybe you're in an emotional summer when it is literally winter outside. This is fine; it happens all the time. How or why would this occur? Life happens. Maybe during winter, you win the lottery; this would toss your emotions and mind straight into the summer season. There are endless scenarios within life that can cause you to be in a different season in your life than the season that the calendar tells you. Learn from the literal seasons, but recognize what season you are in emotionally, mentally, and spiritually, and take care accordingly.

SIX

The Medicine Wheel

Broadly, medicine wheels have been around for ages in all tribes, not only the Native American tribes; moreover, European tribes, African tribes, Australian tribes, the tribes within Asia, etc. Depending on the population's location, medicine wheels may differ from one another. Other things that can impact a medicine wheel are belief systems, cultural expressions, societal norms, what is available to a tribe, and how a person or tribe views the world around them. A medicine wheel can be assigned to a nation, a clan, a family, and an individual. I am going to encourage you to create your own individual medicine wheel from your own worldview and belief system. You can create one on the land and work with the stone nation, or you can simply draw it on a piece of paper. It is up to you—it is yours.

Everything moves through cycles and seasons. The medicine wheel can show you how to apply the concepts of cycles and seasons to your daily life in order to create balance and harmony within yourself and the world around you. There is proof that people have been working with some form of the medicine wheel since the rise of man. One example is from the Neolithic period: the mysterious Stonehenge.

Stonehenge is one of the greatest mysteries in Britain. Although this structure was formed about five thousand years ago, people are still uncovering all of the mysteries of Stonehenge. However, we have seen that Stonehenge aligns with the passing of time in relation to the sun, moon, and stars. The stones were placed precisely in order to record and predict the rising and setting of the sun, moon, and stars.

Stonehenge can be aligned with the solstice and the changing of time. Aligning a wheel with the movement of the sun and other celestial bodies allows us to draw in those energies into our lives. As we rotate around the sun, the seasons on Earth change. This impacts planting, growing, and harvesting, which has a great impact on our daily lives both physically and metaphorically. For example, there is a time to plant new ideas, grow these ideas, and reap the harvest from the initially planted ideas. If you can align the planting, growing, and reaping within your life to the rhythm of the sun and seasonal changes, it only exemplifies the energy of what you are doing. Why? One simple reason would be that the natural world teaches us many things about how to grow, when to grow, and what is necessary for growth in order to harvest. It amplifies the energy represented in the natural world with the energies that we work with in our daily lives. Stonehenge was a type of medicine wheel that could reveal to us the cycles and patterns within the natural world.

Side note, if you are invited into someone else's sacred space (i.e., their circle of friends or their community), you may want to inquire about their traditions and perspective. As a rule of thumb, I respect every circle that I come into in order to gain and grow from that circle's perspective and the wisdom it carries. Even though I may or may not agree with their belief systems and/or methods, as my ideas may differ, it is an opportunity to walk in another person's shoes for a moment. I believe that we are all here to have our own ideas, and the grand circle of humankind should accept that.

That being said, I am going to walk us through many basic ideas and concepts that you may draw on in order to create your personal medicine wheel. However, before I do, we should look at why a person or group of people would want to work with a medicine wheel.

The medicine wheel is a circle. Although the circle is a basic, simple shape, it can represent so much. It is a shape that doesn't have a beginning or an end. It is ever flowing with balance and harmony. There are so many examples of this within nature. On a macro level, we see circular spheres in the planets. On a micro level, we see circles within cells and atoms. Nature flows in these never-ending cycles. Circles make up our world and provide us with a sense of balance and equality. They bring us into a connected flow. Squares have sharp corners, but circles flow smoothly. Circles represent oneness and wholeness. They are encapsulating yet can be expansive. Just like circles, medicine wheels incapsulate all energies and balance these energies together.

When we apply circles to our lives, they represent the never-ending expression of life force. One example of this is the symbol of the wedding ring. Another example is when people congregate in a circle, there is no head of the table, so to speak. All are equally important—it creates a sense of fairness and visual equality within

a group. Each person represents a position, even if they are oppos-
ing sides. It is balanced. Think about communities sitting around
a fire; the community forms a circle. Mankind has recognized this
pattern since the beginning of time.

In sacred geometry, there is a concept called nature's first pattern. The pattern of the universe. It all begins with a center point,
the point from which all things come and where all things will
return. The center point with an equal radius creates a circle.

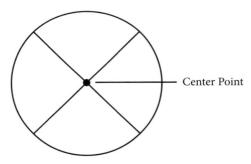

The Center Point

One of the main concepts of the medicine wheel is to consciously maintain a center point within ourselves, those who
surround us, our activities on a day-to-day basis, and our life as
a whole. From a micro level to a macro level and everything in
between, medicine wheels help you seek balance in the unification
of your life.

At times life can knock us off balance; this is normal. But it is up
to you to find your personal balance within your life. My balanced
life may look very different from your balanced life; it is a very individual structure. My social or financial balance may look different
than yours. My family's balance may look different from your family's balance. The point is to find your circle and find your personal

center point in order to stay in balance. This is what the medicine wheel can assist us with.

The medicine wheel provides you with the knowledge of the cycles within your individual life, your family, your community, and mankind as a whole. Although we will be working with a basic four-point wheel, it is good to note that some may have an eight-point wheel, a seven-point wheel, or even a twelve-point wheel depending on their culture, belief system, or what resonates the most with their understanding of the world around them. Medicine wheels can be created with endless opportunities depending on how you view the world around you. I will provide you with some basic information that many belief systems align with; however, not all belief systems do. Remember to continue to think outside the box.

There are many aspects of the medicine wheel that can assist us with our lives on Mother Earth. Although different tribes may interpret the wheel in unique ways, there are some very noticeable aspects that can naturally be recognized by all mankind: the sacred wheel walks us through stages of life, seasons of the year, elements of nature, and more.

Seasons are a type of cycle; however, there are many more types of cycles. A cycle can be defined as a series of events that happen in a specific order and repeat themselves. Hence, there is a pattern. From one perspective, a circumstance may look chaotic, but from a different circumstance, one may realize the circumstance holds a pattern, maybe even a cycle. Some cycles serve us; some cycles harm us. It is good to consider the individual and group cycles that we are in in order to gain a deeper understanding of these cycles. We can then consider if the cycle is working or not. Would you like to add something to the cycle, delete something from the cycle, or revamp the cycle completely? Awareness of your cycles in your life is essential if you would like to consciously change the cycle.

Some cycles are seasons, as mentioned above. This is a good example of a longer cycle. Some cycles are very short and may be experienced within one day. For example, in the morning I wake up and start my day, I eat lunch at noon, I begin to relax in the evening, and at nighttime, I rest. I repeat this cycle every day. We can superimpose the concept of the day into our lifetime.

Things to Add to Your Medicine Wheel

There are layers upon layers of meaning within the medicine wheel. It seems simple; however, it can be extremely dynamic as we move through these layers to align our lives. Below is a short list of what one might find on a medicine wheel.

Direction	Element	Day	Year	Life
East	Air	Morning	Spring	Birth
South	Fire	Noon	Summer	Adolescence
West	Water	Evening	Autumn	Adult
North	Earth	Night	Winter	Elder

Items on a Medicine Wheel

Notice the similarities and the flow between the directions, the element, the time of day, the time of year, and the time within our lives. The themes in each of these concepts can open up your understanding of where you are and what you can work with. The system above is widely worked with; however, it is good to note that some tribes will work with other arrangements. However, this is a basic list that reveals the cycles and systems that we live in from a micro to a macro level. Additional elements can be added to this wheel.

The Four Directions

The four directions—east, south, west, and north—are an important part of many medicine wheels. In order to acclimate oneself, it is good to be aware of these directions from your position. Additionally, if you would like to mark each of these directions on the medicine wheel, feel free! The four directions provide us with longitude and latitude in order for us to find our position on Mother Earth, especially when we are up in the air. Longitude lines travel north and south and latitude lines travel east to west, providing us with coordinates within our lives.

Most medicine wheels follow the basic pattern of having a center of stone(s) with an outer ring of stones and "spokes" (lines of rocks) radiating from the center to the clockwise cardinal directions (east, south, west, and north). These stone structures may or may not be called "medicine wheels" by the people whose ancestors built them; they may be called by more specific terms in that nation's language. The art of intentionally erecting massive stone structures as sacred architecture is a well-documented activity of ancient monolithic and megalithic peoples. These cycles, seasonal cycles, hold us globally as well as culturally.

We align the medicine wheel with the four directions in a clockwise manner: east, south, west, and north. Clockwise movement is also known as sunwise. Why? Well, let's take a step back and look at our orientation to the sun. The sun rises in the east and sets in the west. So, we begin in the east. In the Northern Hemisphere, as the season moves from the summer solstice to winter solstice, the sun leans to the south, making our days shorter and our nights longer as it has a shorter radius within the sky from east to west. As the seasons shift from the winter solstice to the summer solstice, the sun leans to the north once again. Following this pattern of the sun, we see that a person working with a medicine wheel may start in the east, where the sun rises, and move to the south, as it leads us from summer to winter. We then move to the west, where the sun sets, and move to the north, as it leads us from winter into the bright, shiny summer solstice once again.

If you like this idea, aligning structures with directions and the sun can be implemented into a daily practice. For example, maybe you place your bed's headboard so it is facing east. Facing east in the morning and recognizing the significance of the east assists with directing your consciousness to align with the natural world. In a traditional Navajo dwelling called a hogan, the structure's door is always placed in the east. This is so a person would be able to greet the sun in the morning at its dawning. It is said that if you look out across the land in the early hours of the morning, you will be able to see the ancestors dancing in the light. Focusing your consciousness on the bigger picture and connecting with those who have paved the way for you to be here can start a day with gratitude and purpose. In another Native tradition, it is said that once the light of the sun touches you, it is good to speak your day. For example, say if you would like a day of peace, or a day of strength, or a day of productivity, etc. However, if the sun touches you and you do not speak, you will have a day without your voice being heard.

Other Things for Your Wheel

- The four elements can be placed on your medicine wheel—earth, air, fire, and water.
- Time can be placed on the circle—from days to a lifetime.

- Seasons can be arranged on a medicine wheel as well.

- You can also incorporate the four bodies of existence: the physical, emotional, mental, and spiritual bodies; the center point would represent all bodies combined in balance.

- Even animals can be placed here, whether they are four-leggeds, winged ones, water nation, or creepy-crawlies.

- You can add colors for each section to assist them with coming alive.

These are some of the main items that can start you on the path of creating your own medicine wheel.

Designing Your Medicine Wheel

Decide how you will be crafting your medicine wheel. Feel free to use your creativity and imagination. Medicine wheels can be small or large; the size is up to you and what works best in your situation. Will you be drawing it on a piece of paper? That works great if you don't have other resources. If you love to paint, a medicine wheel would be a great pattern to paint in order to recognize the flow. Meditate on the painted medicine wheel; how does it speak to you? If you have space indoors or out, you can sit and create a medicine wheel around you. Sitting in a medicine wheel can rebalance your energy. Perhaps you would like to make one in nature with items such as stones or twigs. I know a family that planted their flower bed in the shape of a medicine wheel (a circular shape, divided into four equal flower beds). If you work with altars and/ or enjoy building your own altar, a medicine wheel would be a perfect model to ensure the balance of the energies on your altar.

If you are creating your medicine wheel on land, work with the natural directions—place the north in the north, etc. Under many belief systems, an individual or group would create a life-size medicine wheel. One would then enter their medicine wheel from the east and only move through it clockwise in a natural flow. This is not to say that all belief systems see it this way; some hail the north. In that case, you may enter from the north side of the medicine wheel. Creating your own medicine wheel is a wonderful exercise. So where do we begin?

Let's begin in the east. The east is where the sun rises. This heralds a new day, a new beginning. In many belief systems, the east aligns with the element of air, and air aligns with thoughts and the mental body. Additionally, air can align with the winged ones; if you wish, represent your favorite winged one in the east. Regarding the seasons, the east holds the spring due to the concept of the newness of time and the burgeoning of the natural world. One could also understand this to be the beginning of life, or birth. Additionally, we could align this with the morning, which brings us right back to the sun rising in the east. This is the time of newness. Choose whichever color you'd like to represent these things to you. I like yellow, but you may choose another color. Depending on the color that you choose, there are many ways that you could work that color into your medicine wheel. For example, if you are drawing or painting your medicine wheel, you may want to depict your chosen color in that quarter of the wheel. If you are creating the wheel around you, you may find something to represent that color (a stone or a flower with petals of your chosen color, for example). Use your imagination! One of the reasons that a medicine wheel is so healing is that you are creating it with your personal meaning. Hence, it resonates with you as an expression of self.

Next, move to the south. The south represents midday. In many belief systems, the south aligns with the element of fire, and fire aligns with action and the spiritual body. Additionally, both fire and the south can align with creepy-crawlies. Remember that creepy-crawlies are insects, reptiles, and amphibians; decide if you would like to include any creepy-crawlies in your medicine wheel. The season for the south is summertime, when the natural world expands and grows. This could directly relate to adolescence, youth, the sensation of vitality. What color does this feel like to you? I like the color red. Up to you. Again, if you are drawing or painting your medicine wheel, work with your chosen color. If you are creating a larger medicine wheel, find objects that represent that color and / or energy.

Now, move to the west. The west represents evening because the sun sets in the west. The west aligns with the element of water and the water nation. What water nation animal speaks to you? You may wish to place it here. The west also aligns with autumn, when the days become shorter and the natural world begins to prepare itself for the sleep of the winter months. As you might guess, this relates to adulthood, a time of maturity and preparation for retirement and harvesting. Because of the element of water, I like using blue here. What color speaks to you?

Finally, we find ourselves in the north. The north represents nighttime. The natural world can be seen as falling asleep or going dormant; hence, this could be considered winter. The north directly aligns with the element of earth, and earth aligns with the physical world and the physical body. The four-leggeds are directly aligned with the earth, so place your favorite four-legged here if you choose. With the slowing down of this part of the medicine wheel, it only makes sense that the north holds sacred space for the elders. Elders, like the winter, have prepared their whole lives to be here. What color speaks to you? I like black because of the darkness of the night. Choose your color; make it your own.

Example of a Medicine Wheel

These are some examples of how to place things on a medicine wheel. I would like to reiterate that there are many different teachings around the medicine wheel, and they depend on a person's worldview. There are many wise concepts from different tribes that have been handed down from generation to generation. I honor each and all of these as we metaphorically sit in the sacred circle together. There may be some that disagree or that sit on the opposite side of the circle from me. This is good; this is valid; this is the way of the circle.

Using Your Medicine Wheel

So now that you understand the concept of the medicine wheel, how do you work with it in your life? There are many ways to work with the medicine wheel. It is often used to manifest.

Here is an example of working with the wheel to manifest something. In the east, come up with an idea or thought. In the south, take action on this thought through research and by grounding the idea. In the west, place your emotions into this working and begin to get even more connected to it. Finally, in the north is where the original thought manifests.

One very effective way to manifest is to create your medicine wheel specifically for what you would like to manifest. Add words or phrases that embody your desire in the east. In the south section, you could write the actions that you need to take to make your dreams come to fruition. In the west, write down how this desire makes you feel; put some emotion into it. And in the north, much like a vision board, place pictures of what you are manifesting. Place your manifestation medicine wheel in a special spot and revisit it occasionally. Feel free to add to it as you begin to manifest, as it may change a little. This is a wonderful way to keep you on track to fulfilling your goals.

If you would prefer to manifest using a life-size medicine wheel, face or stand in the east and consider your desire. Write it down. Next, face the south or stand in the south quadrant and consider the steps that you will take to bring your dreams to fruition. Write the steps down. Turn west or stand in the west and write down how this desire makes you feel. Turn or move to the north and visualize the desire being manifested. Write down how this will make you feel. Be creative with this process; it is from creativity that we manifest new ideas.

Medicine people will work with the cycles and season to connect with the vital, energetic forces that each cycle and season holds. There are numerous ways to work with the medicine wheel; everything rolls in circles, nature rolls in cycles, and so do we.

As a rule of thumb, move through the medicine wheel clockwise—unless you are trying to undo something; then you can move through it counterclockwise. For example, if you are trying to undo a project, start in the north—the end point—where the project was made manifest, and move to the west to examine your emotions around what was created. Next, you move to the south to take action on disassembling, and finally, the project is back in the east with an idea. You can start from square one if you wish to reassemble (or not). However, for the most part, move clockwise with your medicine wheel, the same way the sun travels around the earth.

Medicine wheels encapsulate all energies and balances these energies together. For example, the concepts of life, death, and rebirth are here. Medicine wheels contain the energy of seeking, holding, and releasing. In the first part of life, we seek. We may seek a mate, a career, a home, a family, etc. In the middle of life, we hold and sustain that which we sought after. In the latter part of life, we learn to let go and release. This is the way of nature. In the spring it seeks, in the summer it holds and sustains, and in the fall it releases. Some of us are really good at seeking, some are really good at sustaining, and some are good at letting go. To live a balanced life, we must learn how to do all three at certain points. When you stand or visualize yourself in the middle of your actual or metaphoric medicine wheel, you stand among everything. This is the way of the natural world.

Relationships & Romance

The natural world is our eldest wisdom teacher. It not only shows us how to relate to ourselves and the world around us, but it also shows us how to work with all energy within the medicine wheel. How then can we work with the medicine wheel in regard to relationships and romance? There are many ways to do this! I will provide some thoughts and concepts; however, my hope is that you will develop more for your life.

When you are looking at the medicine wheel within a relationship, you must recognize that the relationship has a medicine wheel of its own. At times one person will swing toward one polarity and the other person will swing to the opposite in order to maintain balance within the relationship itself. Rejecting the idea of polar swings is silly; polar swings are natural within a relationship, especially at the beginning of the relationship. Finding common ground is finding the center.

First, pick a relationship that you would like to understand more. Is this relationship new, in the east of its connection? Is it fresh? Is it just starting to grow? Are their many ideas of what this relationship could be? Have you not had enough time to bring those ideas to fruition? This is a wonderful season of spring, and the burgeoning of the relationship is here. If your relationship is in the east, this is the time to plant that which you want to harvest later. This is the time to work with the winged ones to rise up and take note of the relationship's vision. Plant and nurture the relationship, because from here it will grow and become what you will partake of later. Keep it light and sunny, with plenty of water (emotion). This is the time to set the tone of your relationship. This is the time to set the pace.

Maybe your relationship is on the south side of the medicine wheel. The summer of a relationship is a time of social invitations, creative pursuits, and joy. Summer is the time to grow in the warmth of the sun. The fiery passion of this time will grow what will be harvested later. This is the time of working together, like some of the creepy-crawlies do, in order to get things accomplished. This part is fun and exciting.

Maybe your relationship is in the west. It is harvesttime. Whatever was planted is now ripe for the picking. This is a good time to take stock in what the relationship is and how it is working for each of you. Do you like the harvest? Is the harvest enough to hold your relationship through the winter? Do you want to plant something different next spring? Healthy relationships continuously flow through the medicine wheel. There are continuous discoveries within a relationship, just like in your individual life. Whether good or bad, the harvest is here. This is the time to see what has manifested. It may be time to let go of ideas and/or old patterns. It may be time to hunker down for the winter, comfortably so, or time to solidify what is happening in your relationship to ensure that you both are on the same page. Was this relationship here for just a season, and now that season has come to an end?

A relationship that is in the north is experiencing a little more distance between the partners. This is neither good nor bad; it just is. There is more individuality within the relationship, and at times it may even look a little cold, but the relationship can be solid enough to handle this. I suppose it depends on what seeds were planted and what harvesttime brought. If harvesttime was plentiful, it will carry the relationship through the winter. This is the place of solidity and self-discovery within the relationship or even by yourself. What seeds do you want to plant next spring? As with the medicine wheel, spring will return again.

Difficulties can occur within a relationship when one person is in one season and the other person is in a different season. If one person within the relationship is in the summer and the other is experiencing winter, one of them will want to grow and talk and be close, whereas the other will want to hibernate and become docile. This is usually temporary. However, the one who is in the summer may become offended when their partner does not want to talk or exhibit warmth. As long as partners respect and understand what season the other is in, a relationship can naturally move through these times. This is where communication comes in handy.

Additionally, let's say that one person is in the spring and the other is in fall. This is the type of relationship where one will want to make plans and start something new, whereas the other will want to wrap things up and let go. This is yet another combination that can confuse the relationship if not correctly understood.

This leads us to review the other combinations as well:

- If one person is in the spring and the other is in the summer, the one who is in the spring may feel like the one who is in the summer is moving a little too quickly in the relationship. The springtime partner may need a moment to catch up with all of the summertime partner's plans. The one who is in the summer may wonder what is taking the other so much time to warm up—well, they are simply coming back to life.

- If one person is in the summer and the other is in fall, this could lead to the type of relationship where the summertime partner is not ready to let go and the harvesttime partner is wanting to slow down and prepare for winter.

- If one person is in the fall and the other is in winter, the harvesttime partner may think that the wintertime partner is getting cold, and the wintertime partner may think that the harvesttime partner is too active.

- If one person is in the winter and the other is in spring, the springtime partner may need to adjust their expectations of the wintertime partner and not take things personally, since the wintertime partner is still asleep.

We all flow through seasons individually. The keys to a balanced relationship, if the seasons do not align, are communication and understanding what season your partner is in. Maybe the timing for the relationship is a little off. Understanding and patience can work miracles. If the relationship is aligned, things will flow easily. Even healthy relationships can feel a little stagnant at times; this is merely winter. The key is to make it through the winter; do not allow the winter to take over your relationship.

Moreover, it is good to understand—or at least become aware—that some individuals roll through their season faster than others. Someone might take years to roll through a season or may actually get stuck in one season for an extended amount of time. Let's say that an individual gets hurt within a relationship, or many different types of relationships, over their lifetime; it would be easy to understand that this individual may decide to hibernate in the winter when it comes to future relationships. At this point, they may need outside assistance to move through this season. Yes, I am recommending seeking good counsel if you are stuck in a season. Some may not want to leave the winter, and I respect this, as it is their experience and I may not always understand what caused them to live there. Seasons flow, and we can flow with them and learn from them if we pay attention to the natural world.

So, how do we know what season we are in or know what season another is in? Listen to the self and others. Listen to the words that are selected when describing things. If words like "planning," "ideas," or "new" are used, I would guess spring. If words like "growing," "maturing," or "fun" are used, I would guess summer. If words like "letting go," "moving on," or "releasing" are used, I would guess fall. If words like "downtime," "break," or "maybe later" are used, I would guess winter. Listen to the word choice that someone uses in everyday conversation and you can take a pretty good guess where they are within any given situation.

I would also like to mention that an individual can be in multiple seasons at one time. Maybe at work, they are in the spring, and in a relationship, they are in the winter. This is more common than what you would think. However, keep in mind that aligning yourself with the seasons will explain how to walk through each of these seasons and will balance them out. It is about awareness, and action is taken once awareness is achieved.

There is another type of medicine wheel that can be beneficial with regard to relationships; I call it the listening wheel. There is a variety of people in your life. Using the listening wheel is a practice of prioritizing these individuals within your life. This is also a practice of healthy boundaries. As you prioritize, you begin to understand what is most important to you … and what isn't.

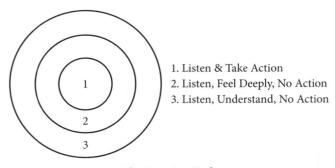

1. Listen & Take Action
2. Listen, Feel Deeply, No Action
3. Listen, Understand, No Action

The Listening Circle

✛✛✛ EXERCISE 11 ✛✛✛
Listening Circle

I invite you to draw a circle on a piece of paper. This is your own listening circle. In the circle, or circle number one, place the names of the people who are the most important to you. These are the people whose words spring you into action. Please make sure that your own name is a part of the inner list!

Draw a second, larger circle around the first circle. Fill the ring with the names of the people whose words may move you emotionally, but whose words you don't take immediate action on, if you take any action at all.

Finally, draw a third, larger circle around the first two circles, adding another ring. In this ring, write the names of those whose words you may understand, but that don't bring you to take action at all.

Note that the names in your listening circle may change throughout your lifetime. Some names will be added; others may move circles/priority.

Here is my personal example of how the listening circle works. If I am in a meeting and I get a message that my husband needs me, I will politely dismiss myself and tend to him because he is in my first circle. However, if I am in a meeting and I get a message that a friend or acquaintance from the second circle is in need, I will be deeply concerned, yet I will continue with the meeting and postpone connecting with my friend until after the meeting. Finally, if I am in a meeting and I find out that something has happened to a stranger in my third circle that I am not in direct contact with, I will feel for them and possibly understand their plight; however, I won't necessarily do anything. This may sound a little harsh to some, but these are my priorities and healthy boundaries.

On the other hand, situations and events may directly change this priority list. If I witness an accident, even if I do not know the person or people involved, I will spring into action and try to assist. This is to say that sometimes our circles change and adapt to the environment.

Putting together your listening circle may be eye-opening as you discover your priorities and boundaries. Are you stretched too thin? If so, simply rebalance your circles and move forward. There are those in our lives that benefit from us making them a priority; hence, the balance within the relationship.

Business & Finance

The first way to examine the medicine wheel within the business world is to have a general understanding of the business cycle itself. In my undergrad programs, I learned the basic business cycle, which includes four parts: expansion, peak, contraction, and trough. Here is a graph that is most commonly used in order to depict this cycle.

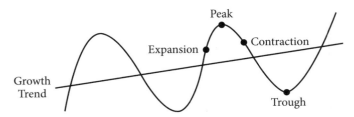

The Standard Business Cycle

The business cycle is not placed in a circle; I wonder if that is because most businesses have a beginning and an end. Or maybe it is because they can depict an upward growth trend. Whatever the reason, I'm going to invite you to look at the business cycle from another position. What if we put the business cycle in a medicine wheel? This would visually place the business cycle as an ongoing system—a system in which all things are natural. A system where we must seek the middle in order to establish balance. A system that we could work with that we already understand, thanks to the natural world, and apply to our business world. The business wheel shows us that there is a time when we need to strategically plan whether we are going to expand or compress the circle. It's simply a different way to look at the world.

In business, the time of expansion is a time of making more money. There are plenty of jobs, we begin to invest more, the economy is improving, etc. To me, this sounds like the spirit of the east—the sun is coming up. It also sounds like spring because this is the time when we plant our seeds. It is morning, and we have a full day ahead of us.

The business term "peak" reminds me of the spirit of the south: the time of movement; the time when the sun is at the peak of the sky; the time of summer and growth.

The Business Cycle in a Medicine Wheel

The business term "contraction" seems like the spirit of the west: the evening time when we began to head indoors to rest. The harvesttime of autumn when we begin to separate our harvest into what we eat during the winter and what we will plant next spring.

Finally, the business term "trough" reminds me of the spirit of the north: the time that we withdraw, as it is night and dark outside. This is not a time to grow—it is the winter. It is time to go within and review the past cycle to see what works and to adjust what doesn't. This is a good time for a business to take inventory and to have a strategic planning meeting to see if it is in the position to expand its circle. Does the business need to contract instead?

When we look at the business cycle through the medicine wheel, it seems more natural that we grow at times and at other times we slow down. This is a lot less frightening than the economic terms "inflation," "recession," and "depression." At times we've wished to blame one person or an industry for difficult changes. However, these things are bound to happen at one point or another. Yes, there are people in positions of leadership that are able to adjust the timing of each of these seasons, but these seasons will happen regardless—this is what the natural world shows us. This is the energy of the cycle and the natural world. How this energy is revealed within each of our lives and stories may differ; however, the cycle of the medicine wheel flows in this pattern. Trust it.

✦✦✦ EXERCISE 12 ✦✦✦
Finances

]This wisdom can be applied to an economy, an industry, a business, or your own personal finances. Work with the wisdom of awareness. Maybe you are in a growth time financially (summer) but others are experiencing the winter. This may be a good time to loan others money, and they can repay you when they make it through their winter (with a little interest). If you are in the winter, hang in there. The natural world teaches us that spring is on the way.

There are many different combinations, as you can see. I invite you to take a moment and consider where you are at within each of these scenarios. My hope is that it will provide you with inner wisdom and help you move forward in kind.

Another way to implement the wisdom of the medicine wheel in business and projects is through the teachings of the butterfly. Working with the medicine wheel to manifest something that you desire is the process of transformation.

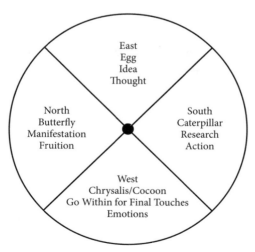

The Butterfly Manifestation Medicine Wheel

In the east, the butterfly would be in the egg stage. The egg stage represents an idea that you may have. The idea holds within itself the potential to become something beautiful. This comes as a thought; remember, thoughts are like wind and the element of air.

Next comes south and the caterpillar. This is the stage of research and growth as the caterpillar gains and grows with all its feet on the ground. An idea begins to grow and take shape. This takes a lot of action—remember, actions are kin to the element of fire.

The west is the chrysalis or cocoon stage. This is when we go within and decide the final touches of the project. In this space within the medicine wheel, we feel into the project with our emotions. Remember, emotions are aligned with the element of water.

Finally, here comes the north—the manifested butterfly. If we have an idea, it begins within the mental realm. Next, we take action on the idea with research. Then we place more emotion and passion around the idea so that we can decide the final touches, and finally the idea becomes manifest in the physical realm. Although we are working with a butterfly, we are also extracting the energy of the four directions, the four seasons, and the four elements. Add anything else that you would like to your own manifestation medicine wheel. Make it your own.

Now I would like to shift gears again. We looked at the business cycle on the medicine wheel. We also looked at the manifestation cycle within the medicine wheel. At this point, I would like to shift to how teams work and don't work in business—hopefully, working with the medicine wheel will improve teamwork.

Dialogue

In the introduction of this book, we touched on the word "dialogue" and how we can dialogue with the natural world. I would like to return to the concept of dialogue and apply it to teams and/or groups of individuals. Dialogue is the art of thinking and reasoning together rather than separately.[26] This type of practice has the ability to draw upon a group mind. It feels like an additional consciousness comes into the group. Have you ever been in a situation where a group of individuals was brainstorming? All of a sudden, an idea appears to the collective and everyone walks out of that meeting not necessarily understanding who came up with the idea. In those moments, it can be seen as the dynamic of group consciousness coming to fruition. I enjoy brainstorming with a good group of people. Although the final idea may come out of my mouth or another's, I recognize that it came due to the dialogue within a group. Now, we are going to look at how dialogue creates trust within a group and for its leader, and finally the ancient world and how our ancestors worked with dialoguing in a circle.

When dialogue occurs within a group, a sense of trust and inclusion is present. During Bohm's exploration of dialogue, he traveled through Europe and North America giving seminars. In 1984, at a seminar in England, Bohm wrote about an observation he made.[27] The seminar began with agendas, lectures, and content; however, something more momentous occurred—a dialogue began to take form and the free flow of meaning was present among all participants.

---

26. Bohm and Weinberg, *On Dialogue*, xviii.

27. Bohm and Weinberg, xix.

The group had no preestablished purpose; at each moment the purpose was free to change and reveal itself. The group thus began to engage in a new dynamic relationship in which no speaker was excluded and in which no particular content was excluded. Thus far we have only begun to explore the possibilities of dialogue in the sense indicated here, but going further along these lines would open up the possibility of transforming not only the relationship between people, but the very nature of consciousness in which these relations arise.[28] In the earlier stages of a group meeting together, people may not trust each other; however, if the group continues to meet and have dialogue, the group will begin to trust each other. Through dialogue, trust is built.

Trust is important to leaders, as trust inspires people to follow a leader. From 2005 to 2008, Gallup conducted a formal study to explore why people follow. One goal was to gain an understanding of the average person's opinion about leadership.[29] This study took a truly random sampling of more than ten thousand followers. These followers were asked the following question: "What leader has the most positive influence in your daily life?" Once the individual had a leader in mind, the following question was posed: "Now, please list three words that best describe what this person contributes to your life." The results of this study revealed that "followers have a very clear picture of what they want and need from the most influential leaders in their lives: trust, compassion, stability, and hope."[30] Trust (trustworthiness) was at the top of the list. Trust is not only essential to organizations and leaders—trust is the number one thing that followers need and look for in a leader.

---

28. Bohm and Weinberg, *On Dialogue*, xix.

29. Rath and Conchie, *Strengths Based Leadership*, 80.

30. Rath and Conchie, 81.

Gallup's research on trust in leadership suggests that the foundation of trust in leadership is closely tied to employee engagement. Additionally, Gallup's national polls indicate that the chance of an employee engaging at work when the employee doesn't trust the organization's leaders is one in twelve.[31] Employees who trust the leaders of an organization are more likely to engage in work.

Although the foundational basis for dialogue provided above applies to the late 1900s, dialogue is an ancient tradition and is still practiced in many cultures around the world. According to Isaacs, "[Dialogue] is both something we already know how to do and something about which there is much to learn. On the one hand, the tradition of dialogue [has a long history; for example, it] can be traced to the talking circles of the Native Americans, to the *agora*— or marketplace—of ancient Greece and beyond that to the tribal rituals of many indigenous people in Africa, New Zealand, and elsewhere."[32]

Here is an example of a traditional model of dialogue from a Native American tribe, which is still in practice today: the Navajo Nation practices a working model of dialogue in order to sustain a peaceful future for their culture. This model is known as Peacemaker Court; it is used to resolve the tribal dispute through dialogue and is recognized as Tribal Sovereignty in the United States.

In a typical peacemaking session, participants sit in a circle, sometimes with a lit candle in the middle. The Navajo call this process "talking things out." Unlike a state or federal court, peacemaking does not follow rules of evidence, does not look for an objective truth, and does not focus on blame. Emotions play an important role in the conversation; participants' feelings are valued

---

31. Rath and Conchie, 83.

32. Isaacs, *Dialogue and the Art of Thinking Together*, 24.

as much—if not more—than reason. After the discussion has been exhausted, the peacemaker may discuss religious values, the tribe's value system, and previous cases that resemble the current dispute. He or she may offer guidance on moving forward. The ultimate goal is a consensus resolution to restore relationships and alleviate suffering.

In this model, participants sit in a circle, and each individual speaks. Everyone else in the circle listens. This process occurs until every member of the circle who would like to speak has had the opportunity to do so. The goal of this model is to establish a consensus, and it promotes a community of those involved. In addition to the Navajo Nation, there are many Native American tribes with a Peacemaker Court in place, including Choctaw Nation, Seneca Nation, the Northern Arapaho Tribe in Wyoming, and the Eastern Shoshone Tribe in Wyoming. This type of dialogue assists the Native American community in dispute resolution by respecting their ancient tradition of a circle of community dialogue.

Additionally, ancient civilizations in Europe displayed practices of gathering in groups to speak with each other—this is dialogue. The ancient Greeks had a commonplace to assemble, as Isaacs mentioned. The gathering place for ancient Romans was called a forum. Throughout history, people have gathered together for the purpose of dialogue.

Health & Well-Being

There are many ways to apply the medicine wheel to our personal health and well-being. We will start with the one that is close to my heart. Traditionally, within the Navajo Nation there is a story of the beginning of time, when all was chaos. There was only a medicine bundle. From this medicine bundle came a brother and sister.

Their hair flowed long and beautiful. They were seen only for one night. That night, they were singing and painting all the life-forms. By the morning, the world as we know it was created. They still exist, although we cannot see them. Their names are Thought and Speech.

In the Navajo Nation, this is the basis for many of the ceremonial rituals that take place, whether the ritual is for healing or celebration. The ritual may have a sand painting and song that will last for days at a time. This is the act of rebalancing, recreating the world as we know it.

If the ritual is performed for an individual, the individual will sit in the middle as a focal point and the artists will create a sand painting around the individual. At times, the sand painting is created prior to the individual sitting in the middle; at other times, the sand painting is created around them. The sand painting will have different colors of sand, which is ground sandstone. The different colors come from the different colors of sandstone within the native land. The colored sand is then trickled through the fingers of artists to land upon a tan background of earth sand. Anyone who wants to participate in the sand paintings can—both young and old, male and female. There may have been certain ceremonies where only a select group of individuals would participate; however, it is my understanding that if you wanted to help, you were allowed to help. This tradition was handed down through generations.

The artists draw a variety of symbols around the individual, which depend on the purpose or focus of the ceremony. Artists work with the understanding of color harmony and contrast within the natural world in order to rebalance the world of the individual. It is cast on one big circle as songs are sung. This all takes place in order to assist that individual to reemerge into life in a balanced way. Once the ceremony is completed, the sand painting is destroyed and taken away from the place it was created. It is disposed of by a spiritual leader. The main reason for this is because it is thought that the negative energy was sucked into the sand itself. The individual is seen to have a rebirth into this life, and all is well within their world.

At times when an individual will experience imbalance, whether physically, emotionally, mentally, or spiritually, the individual will seek out a medicine person who will create a circular sand painting. Although the Navajo may work with sand, other cultures come together in a circle to perform healing work. Hence, it literally is a medicine wheel.

As a little girl, I remember attending events where sand paintings were being made. It was captivating. My father (full-blood Navajo) told me that, initially, different symbols were created in each sand painting in different areas of the Navajo Nation and for different clans. Once the Navajo Nation began to weave blankets, the symbols from sand paintings would translate to the patterns on the blanket. When the Navajo would wear these blankets as cloaks and travel outside of their area, everyone would know where they came from—this was a long, long time ago.

If you are interested, you can purchase sand paintings in the form of artwork; however, they may have different symbols within them.

The Four Bodies

As with other health and well-being sections, we take a step back and consider the four bodies of existence. Have you ever been in a situation where your physical body was in one place, your emotional body was in another, and your mental body was in a different place altogether? I think that when this happens, our spiritual body takes a backseat, as we are not aligned at this time. Maybe you are at work physically, but emotionally you are with your mate or newfound friend. Maybe your mind is thinking about what you may need to pick up at the store on the way home. After a period of time living like this, I began to feel out of place. It makes sense, doesn't it?

Here is another way to approach this topic. Have you ever heard of a Stradivarius? A Stradivarius is a stringed instrument, usually a violin; however, you can find a Stradivarius cello as well. These instruments are one of a kind, authentic, and exquisite. They also are some of the world's most expensive instruments. They cannot be replicated or duplicated. These instruments will retail for millions of dollars. So what if the body of the violin was in one place, the string in another, and the bow and tuning pegs were in a completely different place? What kind of music would it play? Well, as you can image, it wouldn't play any music at all. Although it would have all of the makings to play beautiful music, no sound would emit.

Now, what if you are like a Stradivarius? You are one of a kind, authentic, and exquisite. You are supreme and cannot be duplicated, nor can you be replicated. I believe that each of us is like this—no one can be the vibration and expression of life that you can. Maybe our physical body is like the body of the violin. Our emotional body is the strings. Our mental body is the tuning pegs, and our spirit is the beautiful bow that brings the music out of us. And so it is; we assemble our four bodies of existence and play the expression of life that each of us is. You are authentic, just like me.

Many years ago, I was compartmentalized. I was a single mom of a teenage boy. I worked full-time in an office on the thirty-seventh floor. I was going to school at night. And, to top it off, I was working my way toward receiving my black belt. Sounds like a busy life! Yeah, it was so busy that I couldn't even hear what my soul was saying.

In order to maintain all of these things, I kept them separate from one another. I didn't bring what I was learning in martial arts about balance and breathing to my life. I didn't bring what I was learning in school to the workplace. And, of course, I was Momma Joy-Joy at home, buying pizza for all of the neighborhood kids. I was becoming so tired and thin, compartmentalized. One day the idea come to me about the Stradivarius, and I began to reassemble myself. I began to integrate all of my separate worlds, and I began to become more authentic and whole.

Assemble your physical body with your emotional body. Be where you are. Become mindful of where you are and reconnect with the self. Allow the spirit to express itself through each of your bodies of existence and bring your beautiful music to the world. Place each of your bodies on the medicine wheel and give each of them a voice. Give your emotions permission to have a voice. Give your mind permission to express itself. Find your balance on the medicine wheel and feel whole once again. Be your greatness, as only you can be.

I have experienced and seen in many societies and belief systems that people are denied a voice. I believe that if you give yourself permission to listen to yourself, you gain and grow in consciousness. Know thyself and you will know the universe.

SEVEN
The Shadow Self

Now that we have learned some of the natural world's wisdom and discovered the medicine wheel, I would like to discuss another idea that can improve your life: the shadow. The shadow is alive. Life wants to be recognized. Life wants to be acknowledged. Life wants to be understood. Life wants to be respected. How can this happen if my shadow isn't recognized, acknowledged, understood, or respected? If I see my shadow as bad and/or shameful, it will hide from me. If it hides from me (or me from it), it will exist in a primitive pygmy state. This can lead to tragedy. Awareness brings recognition. Acceptance allows it to be acknowledged. Compassion and curiosity allow it to be understood. And knowing it will bring respect.

Come with me as we approach a very taboo topic—the shadow self. My goal is to approach the shadow from more of an organic, natural position and/or worldview. I am approaching this from an inquisitive mind, from a position of psychology and philosophy, and from a position of wonder.

What Is the Shadow?

Let's take a step back and examine the shadow from the position of psychology and the various perspectives of Freud, Jung, and others. Sigmund Freud is the founder of psychoanalysis and could be considered one of the fathers of psychology. Freud created the concept of the id, the ego, and the superego.[33] He considered these three concepts structures that govern the personality of every human being.

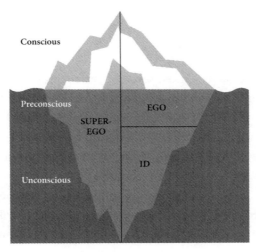

The Id, Ego, and Superego

---

33. Freud, "The Ego and the Id," 5–22.

The personality structure of the id is fully unconscious. This means that the id affects our personality in a way that we are not consciously aware of. The id demands immediate gratification; it wants to gain pleasure, avoid pain, and reduce tension. This is what Freud referred to as the pleasure principle.[34]

According to Freud, the personality structure of the superego is mostly—but not completely—unconscious, as can be seen in the previous figure. The superego subscribes to taking the moral high road, doing well for others, and ideal outcomes.[35] It is described as the moralizing aspect of our mental function. It is similar to what we call our conscience. In order to satisfy this personality structure, we must never think, feel, or do anything wrong. This is what Freud referred to as the moral principle. However, it can lead to an immense amount of guilt and shame. "The superego can be thought of as a type of conscience that punishes misbehavior with feelings of guilt."[36]

The personality structure of the ego is mostly conscious. The ego acts as an intermediary between the superego and the id. The ego will do its best to balance the reality of the id, ego, and superego, and this is referred to as the conscious mind and/or "self" of an individual; moreover, who we perceive ourselves to be. Freud referred to this as the reality principle. The ego is seen as an organized and realistic aspect of self. However, the ego does hold the ability to unconsciously distort our reality as well.

These are concepts to assist us in examining and explaining how the human mind works. From my studies on Freud, his perspective was that the superego should clamp down on and/or destroy the id.

---

34. Freud, "The Ego and the Id," 5–22.

35. Freud, 5–22.

36. CommonLit Staff, "Freud's Theory."

There is an alternative approach to understanding the human mind, created by Carl Jung. When Freud was launching his career, Carl Jung was just a young boy. By the time that Jung became a published author, Freud was widely recognized. They began to converse, but they did not always agree about things such as the unconscious. Freud took the position that the unconscious was a depository for repressed emotions and desires that were deemed unacceptable by the individual; however, Jung believed that the unconscious was a storehouse of memories, not necessarily good or bad, that was both individual and ancestral.[37] Now psychology had a broader base to build upon.

Jung coined the phrase *shadow self.* Throughout his work, he refers to the shadow. According to Jung, the shadow is a darkness that lies within everyone's unconscious mind—an aspect that many find too frightening to face, let alone explore. Jung states that the shadow self can never be defeated; however, it can be tamed.[38] If tamed, it can lead to personal cultivation and the evolution of the mind. The shadow possesses the most inferior characteristics of the psyche, characteristics that are frowned upon by our conscious self and/or our peers within society and civilization. It is facing and embracing the shadow that we are afraid of most. People are afraid to admit what they are truly capable of, especially things that are morally frowned upon.

There is a Latin phrase that Jung would use: *In sterquiliniis invenitur,* which means "in dung, it shall be found."[39] One can become enlightened by bringing the shadow into the light of consciousness. Instead of destroying the id, as Freud would posture, it can

---

37. Jung, *Archetypes and the Collective Unconscious*, 93–94.

38. Jung, 270–72.

39. Jung, *Mysterium Coniunctionis*, 35.

be dissolved and integrated. If the shadow is repressed, it will seep out in disturbing ways. The shadow, by nature, stays hidden to the self so that we may continue to believe with conviction that we are good and moral human beings. It may hide from others so that we can fit in socially and be perceived as just and moral.

Morality

Let's talk about morality. From a philosophical position, morality is a set of rules and/or agreements that we have placed on ourselves and others in order to coexist. Why are there so many cultures with differing views about moral codes? Because of our differences around the globe. How can the moral code continuously be adjusted to be the most beneficial for society? Morals should not be created based on one personal view; they are a code that is agreed upon within a society in order to keep the society functioning. Moral code can change depending on the society. What was once immoral may now be moral and vice versa.

Most people adopt the moral system given to them without questioning or examining it. The moral judgments of good and evil need to be questioned so that we don't find ourselves with a hyper-simplified definition of morality, which would limit ourselves and those around us. "Western mortality has historically been a struggle between elements," according to Nietzsche.[40] Nietzsche was a nineteenth-century German philosopher whose work questioned and challenged universal truths.

Nietzsche states that if we don't examine our moral code, it will create "a smaller, almost ridiculous type, a herd animal, something

---

40. Nietzsche, *On the Genealogy of Morals*, xxi.

eager to please, sickly, and mediocre."[41] In the words of my son, a "sheeple." Nietzsche is not only giving us permission to examine our moral code, but he is also demanding it of us.

So what are we so afraid of? Is it our shadow, or is it that we may not belong in an old, unnatural moral code? I don't know how to answer this question; however, I do hope that I have provided enough food for thought so that you will have the courage to think outside the box, to question, to approach your shadow self, and to become your authentic, whole self.

According to Jung, if we can become conscious and integrate the shadow into our consciousness, we evolve and become whole. We must embrace the shadow, not as an important aspect of one's day-to-day life, but as a necessary and vital part of the complete self. Denying it only makes it worse. However, the shadow not only contains troubling impulses, but also potent, creative, and powerful capabilities. The shadow, once realized, is the source of renewal and positive impulses. Until we meet our shadow side, a part of us remains imprisoned. Embracing the shadow will open to the door to the totality of the self and lead to enlightenment and evolution.

Judgment and Forgiveness

At this point, I would like to briefly approach the concept of judgment and forgiveness. There are many belief systems that tell us that we will meet our judge and jury at the end of our lifetime, the final day of judgment. Some say that if you do not live a good life, your soul will not move through this rite of passage; others say you will return to Earth to have a do-over; still others say you will go to hell. However, if you pass this final test of judgment, you become

---

41. Nietzsche, *Beyond Good and Evil*, 82–84.

immortal or go to heaven, etc. I find this concept interesting, so let's examine it for a moment.

In Egyptian lore, the recently deceased stand before Anubis, the god of the dead, or the god of passage into the underworld. They enter the underworld and face all that they have become, and they must face rawness and monsters. If the deceased is able to traverse this section, they move into Ma'at's hall—Ma'at is the goddess of truth and justice. At this point, the deceased is faced by forty-two assessor gods who must be convinced that they are just and pure. As the deceased moves through this, they work with the energy of "do not stand as a witness against me," which means that your heart will not betray you as you stand in judgment. At this point, Anubis uses a scale to weigh the deceased's heart against the Feather of Ma'at. The heart is viewed as the seat of emotion, memory, and intelligence. If the deceased's heart is as light as a feather, they have successfully completed this rite of passage and will continue to the afterlife.

In Greek lore, the recently deceased are faced by the ferryman of the underworld, Charon, and the river Styx. The ferryman's primary goal is to take the souls of man from the middle world (the land of the living) to the underworld (the land of the dead). The journey is not free; there is a price, the price of a coin. When a loved one died, family would place a coin with the deceased, either in their mouth or on their eyes (I have heard both). The deceased who could not afford to pay the ferryman roam the river for eternity. However, if the ferryman receives his coin, he transports the deceased to the land of the dead. Again, there is a test (or judgment, or price) upon the great transition.

There are many more legends and lore that indicate that people face something at the end of their life that will inevitably hold them accountable for the life that they lived. Judge not lest thou be judged, so to speak.

As I have studied many religions and quite a bit of lore, I question which being the deceased stands before. This is where I stand at this point: I wonder—and you are free to disagree—if we are our own judge and jury. At least for the most part. (I am not taking into consideration sociopaths or psychopaths.) I mean, think about it. We are the hardest on ourselves. I have been harder on myself, with less forgiveness for myself, than I have ever been on another human being. I am the one who knows what I have done and why. I am the one who understands my motives. I understand my mistakes, too. Wouldn't it stand to reason that I am my own judge, determining if my heart is truly light as a feather?

If I am going to judge another person for missing the mark, in my clearest hour, wouldn't I then judge myself against the same scale? Yes, of course I would. So, I then looked at my internal judge and jury and pled my case. I asked for mercy. I asked for forgiveness. At times, I had a pardon; if I can grant others this, I should be able to grant this to myself. I began to forgive others who I thought had tripped up. This isn't to say that I befriended them again—I simply understood that they were human. Hence, I allowed myself to be human. I forgave myself—the hardest person in the world to forgive—and I embraced my humanity. Forgive others, and please forgive yourself. Allow your soul to be free.

At times people may project their shadow onto other people and/or situations. You must recognize when you are doing this in order to stay healthy. For example, once an acquaintence came up to me and said that she needed to apologize to me. I sat with this lady for a minute as she spoke her truth. She told me that she had been judging me and that she was sorry. Without hesitation, I said, "I forgive you."

She had an astonished look on her face. She then asked how I was able to forgive her so quickly without even knowing the details. She told me that she considered me to be a spiritual light person (also known as a lightworker) and thought that I should not be contaminating my vessel with cigarettes or alcohol. She had seen me smoking the other day and then judged me for it.

I again looked at her and said, "I forgive you."

She asked how I could do that so quickly. I explained to her that I did not believe that she was judging me, but that she was judging herself. She then reached into her bag and pulled out a pack of cigarettes.

At times we may project our shadows onto other people, or they may cast their shadow on us. If you are able to recognize this, it will help you stay in balance.

So how can we not take other people's shadow personally? This is a great question, but I can only answer this from my perspective. I invite you to answer this question for yourself as well. When I began to realize the times I projected onto other people, it helped me realize when another projected onto me. The key is for me to recognize when I am projecting first. Then the next step is to recognize when somebody else is projecting onto me. And when I recognize that they are projecting onto me, I'm able to not take it so personally, for projection is a human phenomenon.

How to Approach the Shadow

I want to redefine the shadow and look at it from a different perspective for a moment. What if we looked out into nature and the natural world and saw the shadow from that point of view? It would shift our perspective from looking at the shadow as bad and/or evil. It would shift our perspective from looking at the light as good. It would allow us to look at the shadow for what it is naturally.

Let's start with the shadow of a tree. Do you enjoy having a picnic, reading a book, or meditating under the shadow of a tree? From this perspective, we recognize that everything casts a shadow at one point or another if it is in the light, for it is the light that casts the shadow within nature.

What if the shadow was a self-defense mechanism created by the most primal side of self? Much like the beautiful rose and its thorns. The beautiful rose does not apologize, nor does it hide its thorns. It is the thorns that protect it, a self-defense mechanism created from a primal positioning. This keeps the rose in balance. This allows the rose to be beautiful and protected.

Fight, Flight, or Freeze

There is a primal consciousness that will override the conscious mind. It is the amygdala portion of the brain. The amygdala is the part of the brain that senses fight, flight, or freeze mode within a being. The amygdala gets hot when the body senses that it is in a life-threating situation. It is not an idea or a thought; it is a sense that cannot be controlled. When this happens, the conscious mind escapes the body so that it will not feel the impact of said threat. It will only return when the body senses that it is in a safe environment. Safety is key here. Once the body senses that it is in a safe environment, only then will the consciousness of the right and left hemispheres return and the individual will be able to reconnect with their body.

For example, this phenomenon occurs when a person is in a car accident. Initially, the person will not feel the impact and/or whiplash. When they reflect on the car accident, the person might say that everything went into slow motion. It is likely not until the next day that the neck, head, and/or back will feel sore. This is when the individual begins to feel safe, as they are outside of the situation and within a safer environment. At this point, the consciousness returns in the body. However, once the body feels safe, it will begin to express the adrenaline rush of said accident. The person may begin to freak out at this point, hours after the situation has receded. I have found that a person feels foolish (or is looked upon as foolish) to freak out after the situation has passed; I would encourage the person to express all of their feelings at this point in time. This adrenaline rush is the amygdala cooling itself down, which allows the brain's right and left hemispheres to once again feel the safety within the body. If the person does not complete the cycle by experiencing the adrenaline rush, this could establish a trigger within the primal consciousness. If a person who survived a car accident does not allow themselves to complete the cycle, the next time they drive a car or see something that reminds them of the accident, their amygdala will get hot again and they will re-exit their body. Only when the person expresses their adrenaline rush will the amygdala calm down and will the cycle be complete. I took a class once about this, and it has assisted me to understand this natural cycle.

My Accident

Because I had knowledge about the amygdala and its functions, I was able to apply it to a situation that I was in. An opportunity came for me to go four-wheeling with a group of people. I had never been four-wheeling before, so I thought that it would be a fun experience. I came to find out that I didn't feel safe riding as fast as the others. They were more experienced and knew the terrain—I did not. Soon enough, I began to fall behind the rest of the group. Then I realized that I was so far behind that I couldn't see the rest of them. I didn't want to get lost, so I sped up; I was going faster than I was comfortable with. Soon enough, I drove the four-wheeler into a ditch and flipped over the front.

As I lay there, I was in shock—I felt nothing. I knew that I had been in an accident, so I began to check the rest of my body. Removing my glove, I realized that some of my fingers were disjoined. Instead of getting up or calling for help, I simply laid on the ground for a period of time, hoping the group would return. I am not sure how much time passed, but sure enough, they came back.

At the time, I recognized that my amygdala was in the fight, flight, or freeze mode; I was experiencing the freeze mode. I applied the knowledge that I had from the class that I took. I must have looked so odd to the group as I lay there on the ground, cool as a cucumber.

They asked me if I was okay. I said, "I don't know." I told them that I was in shock and that I was not in the right mind to make any decisions or assess the situation. I spoke with a calm, logical tone, so I am sure I sounded strange. Then I showed them my hand with the dislocated fingers. They told me that I needed to go to the emergency room. But, in order to get there, I needed to get on the back of another person's four-wheeler and ride back to our vehicles. This was a forty-five-minute ride. Talk about getting back up on the horse! Thankfully, I was still in shock, and my left and right hemispheres were hovering outside of my body. We made it to the car, and another forty-five minutes later, I entered the emergency room. Once I was in the care of a kind doctor and nurse, my amygdala must have sensed that I was in a safe environment. I began to shiver and shake throughout my whole body. I asked the nurse if it was cold in the room. He got me some warm blankets and said, "No, it is not cold. You are simply experiencing the adrenaline rush from the experience that you just had."

I must tell you that I felt a little foolish as I laid there shaking and shivering. A thought came to me that I looked silly and that I should stop shaking. Funny how our mind works. However, because of the knowledge that I had, I allowed myself to continue to shake in order to let my amygdala cool down and complete the cycle. My consciousness returned to my body, and I thought how remarkable it was that I could make a sound decision about the situation while I felt like I was hovering over myself; I could only do this because I understood what was going on. If I didn't allow myself to naturally complete this cycle, I would be triggered every time that I saw a four-wheeler. To this day, I have never ridden on another four-wheeler; however, I did ride on the back of my husband's motorcycle for a while, and I doubt that I would have been able to do so if I still had a trigger.

What if the shadow is a defense mechanism created during a traumatic event? What if the shadow gets triggered by odd little things, like a four-wheeler? What if some—if not all—of our shadow side is simply trying to defend itself from re-traumatizing? I am not a psychologist; I am simply a person who has spent years thinking about such concepts. So, I pose the question to you: Do you think that some of your shadow sides came from a traumatic experience?

We all have a shadow. You must accept it and allow it to exist, just like the day allows the night to exist. The approach must be clear with intent. The shadow asks, "Why are you seeking me?" If I respond, "I seek to destroy you!" my shadow will run and hide from me. But it will still exist. It will just become skewed or sideways. There are many ways that the shadow comes out sideways. What I mean by this is when I have a disproportionate response to a given situation—when I overreact. Yes, I admit that I do this at times. When you notice yourself overreacting, this is the time to pose these questions to yourself: What was I feeling? What did I understand about that situation? How did I perceive what was going on? Was there another time within my life that I felt like this? Maybe during my childhood?

This is how you can begin to seek out your shadow and have a dialogue with it. This is your opportunity to allow the shadow (the thoughts and feelings—the senses) to be recognized. This is the time when you are able to move the energy within yourself and complete the cycle with the adrenaline rush in a safe environment. At times, we can work through this on our own. Other times we may seek out a trusted friend or perhaps could benefit from the assistance of a professional. My point is that we all have these experiences; I have never had a conversation with someone who didn't understand the word "trauma." Think about it—it is a natural occurrence. Let's move through this energy together.

Good and Bad

Let's look at nature's law—the rules that nature follows. Let's separate this law from man-made law. "Any concept or force may be divided into two totally opposite concepts or forces, each of which contains the essence of the other. Opposites can be defined only in relation to each other."[42] This is referred to as the law of duality. When we peer into nature, we see many dualities. Nature shows us

---

42. Whitcomb, *Magician's Companion*, 15.

light and dark, day and night, height and depth, cold and hot, etc. This is not to be confused with good and evil.

Good and evil are man-made concepts in order for us to create a moral code so that we may function as a group or society. Natural code can be found in nature. Nature doesn't say that something is good or evil—it is what it is. Yes, things get hurt and die in nature, but man states whether or not that is good or bad. Stating that something is good or bad is a human idea. Nature simply *is*. So, don't separate yourself from what is in your nature. The shadow is natural, as natural as a good night.

At times you may project your shadow self onto another person. You may not be aware that this is what you are doing—it happens. Things that you may not want to face within yourself can become your judgment of others. Moreover, in order for people to believe that we are good, we separate our consciousness from what we perceive as the enemy—or shall I say "the in of me"—within. Shadows can be cast. Make sure that you are not casting your shadow onto another. Embrace it!

Befriending My Shadow

Here is the story of when I began to befriend my shadow consciously. One dark night, I felt my shadow as though it was an entity outside of myself. The moment I looked at her, I began to yell at her, telling her to leave me alone. I expressed to her that she was mean, although I used many more colorful words. I was angry at her and wanted her to leave me alone. She then looked at me and said, "Why do you treat me like this? Why are you so angry with me? I have saved your life on at least five occasions! I love you. I am here to protect you!"

At that moment a clear memory of a past event came to my mind. When I was seventeen years old, one evening I was walking home from the grocery store with both my hands full of groceries. I decided to take a shortcut through a parking lot. Out of nowhere, a man came from behind me. I could smell the alcohol as he whispered in my ear, "I have a knife in your back, and I am willing to use it. You will do exactly what I tell you to do!"

At that moment, something took over me. I remembered that I can naturally whistle so loudly that it hurts my own ears. This whistle is so loud and piercing that it calls bats. So out from my mouth came the screeching, piercing, deafening whistle. As you can imagine, the man let go of me and grabbed his ears. I began to run. I ran all the way home to safety.

An aspect of my shadow self was born at that moment, defending and saving my life from a man who was trying to cross my boundaries in a life-threatening way. My shadow shows up anytime that she senses I may be in danger. Over the years, she has saved my life in situations such as these. However, I have called her colorful names and tried to deny her as a part of me. Why? Because I want to be recognized as a sweet, kind human being. However, this rose has thorns as well.

The problem wasn't that my shadow existed—the problem was that I denied her. And so, she would come out when I least expected her, at times unwarranted. Occasionally she would come out if I perceived that a man wanted to control me and/or cross my boundaries, whether or not that was their intent.

The night that my shadow revealed herself to me, she let me know that she came out of a protection mechanism. She said that she had saved my life on more than one occasion. At this point, I shifted my perspective of my shadow. I fell to my knees and cried in front of her, and when I stood up, I embraced her. I thanked her for all that she had done for me.

And then I let my shadow know that we were safe now. I recognized her and all her power and glory and love for me. I told her that we were with a man that was not going to hurt us. I told her that she could watch over me, but that she did not need to be so defensive because we were in a safe place now. She still exists within me. She is now one of my best friends. She is me.

This aspect of self still speaks with me at night sometimes. She tells me the truth about how I am feeling from another perspective. Recently, she revealed to me that she not only protects me, but that she helps me see my truth no matter how ugly I think it to be. She asks me to examine my life and to see if any man has ever come to my defense before now. The truth is that I cannot recall a time when a man stood up for me or had my back—until now. I know I'm with a man who does not seek to harm me; he will defend me. As she speaks with me, she brings these things into my consciousness, and as sad as they may sound to some, I am happy to know more about who I am and what I have—and have not—experienced. My shadow is my friend.

At times the shadow appears as self-righteousness, condescension, or judgment. Other times it comes out as shame, rebellion, or guilt. I choose to embrace my shadow as a keeper of wisdom, my teacher, my friend. My shadow is alive. When I befriend my shadow, my shadow befriends me.

Anger

I still want to be a nice, kind person. But there are times that I need to feel protected. The side of me that wants to be kind sometimes won't tell me the complete truth of what I am feeling. Does that sound familiar to you? For example, I love to be at peace with other people, but there are times in life when others seek to harm me. And in order for me to be at peace with these people, I must distance myself from them.

All is energy! Energy seeks its freedom. Energy wants to be recognized for what it is. Energy wants to be expressed. When we imprison energy, it suffers and we suffer. When we do not recognize energy for what it is, it is left ignored. When we do not express energy, it is denied. The energy does not disappear. It is simply imprisoned, ignored, and denied. After this energy builds up for a while, it will seek its freedom. It will want you to recognize it—it will want to be expressed. So it may come out sideways, or directed at something else. So it is with the shadow. If I ignore my shadow, it doesn't go away. Instead, it will take over at odd times. Embrace your shadow or it will embrace you.

This is a good space to introduce another concept. I was raised to believe that anger is one of the seven deadly sins. But isn't anger a natural emotion expressed throughout nature itself? Envision a gorilla protecting his family; he looks angry to me. Take a look at a wolf that is protecting its pack. I would like to propose that it is not anger that is deadly as much as it is unexpressed or denied anger. Denied anger does not mean that it goes away—it will simply come out sideways and, for the most part, projected onto the wrong situation.

Historically, I am very uncomfortable with feeling angry. However, anger is a very real thing. It is energy with a purpose. Even in the book *On Death and Dying* by Elisabeth Kübler-Ross, she references anger as a natural emotion. I suppose that I was taught that anger was wrong. But anger is very real. And just because we ignore it doesn't mean that it goes away. Like the shadow, it would like to be expressed and recognized.

I discovered that because I wasn't expressing my anger, it was still there. It was slowly causing a storm to brew within me. I found that moving through the energy of anger can be accomplished in a sacred space without harm to anyone. I also recognized that I wasn't angry at a person—I was simply angry at situations. Even though at times I would blame a person for a situation, it is the situation itself that made me angry. Next time you experience anger, ask yourself if you are angry at a person or at a situation. It is much easier to allow anger when it is directed at a situation and not a person.

For example, I was married at a young age, and had my son when I was twenty years old. There was a lot about life and relationships that I did not understand at that time. I learned the hard way. After twelve years, I divorced my son's father. This was a very difficult time in my life, and there were a lot of things that both he and I got angry about. I remember feeling anger, sadness, disappointment, etc. I allowed myself to feel these feelings without placing them on my son's father. This paid off in very profound ways as I was raising my son because I didn't speak poorly of his father at all. Hence, my son is so much more well-adjusted and was able to build a relationship with his father from his own perspective—not mine. It's a good practice to get angry at situations rather than people. All is energy. Energy likes to be free and not denied. May we learn how to do this in a constructive way.

I Am that I Am

Let me share a story with you that I heard a long time ago. There once lived a man that did a social experiment. He decided to walk around and identify and connect with the things and the people around him in a very profound way to see the interconnectedness of us all. As he was going about his day, he saw a homeless person, and he realized that if life circumstances would have taken him in a different direction, he too could have been homeless. So, in his mind, he looked at the homeless person and said, "I am that." The next day, he saw a wealthy man on Wall Street and realized that if life had taken him in certain directions or provided him with certain opportunities, he could have been that guy on Wall Street as well. So, in his mind, he said, "I am that." Through the course of a year, he began to identify with everyone and every walk of life. And after a year he said, "I am that I am!"

And so it is with the light and the shadow. I am that I am! If given the right circumstances, I recognize within myself that I am the brightest light and the darkest shadow. It is only when we deny our self that we become less whole! I pray that I will be able to continue along this path, becoming more whole through expression and acceptance. And, as I pray this and continue down my path, I will accept all of you, too. Be your greatness, as only you can be!

EIGHT
Empowerment

There are many ways that I like to celebrate the natural world. One of the biggest ways I do this is by paying attention to the seasons. I have a party or do a ritual for the change of the seasons. You can create your own celebration and expression if you wish. I usually invite a group of people to come together and discuss the season. We share food and drink. I always leave a little libation and morsels of food out for the spirits of the land. I remind myself to be aware of who I am and where I am—mindfulness. In chapter 1, we examined this concept. Mindfulness and balance are key to a healthy relationship with self, others, and the natural world.

I also make an effort to recognize the concept of animism— that everything is energy and all energy holds consciousness. This assists me as I work with everything around me in a respectful manner and reminds me to honor where I am, who I am, and all my teachers who helped bring me here. Recognize the wisdom within the natural world. Reminding yourself to be free is empowering. May you be empowered!

The Animal Kingdom

The animal kingdom opens a natural receptor within us. No matter what belief system one may hold or where on the globe one may be, animals hold wisdom for each of us in any given situation. For example, animals are national symbols around the world. The United States of America is symbolized by a bald eagle. The golden eagle is the animal symbol of Egypt, Iraq, Germany, and Mexico, to name a few. The tiger is the animal symbol of India, South Korea, Vietnam, and others.

Additionally, the financial markets are represented by the bull and the bear. Some company logos even have an animal. Sports teams may have an animal mascot or have a name that directly relates to an animal. Automobile companies have named some of their automobiles after animals. Animals show up in legends and lore as well as any given spiritual path. We are aligning with them all the time from around the globe.

Now, I pose the question: Why can't I find a sports team called the snails or a bank with a hyena in the logo? Why can't I find an automobile that is called the turtle? Maybe they are out there, but what kind of message would it relay? We have been connecting with the animal kingdom and applying their attributes to our lives, countries, companies, sports teams, and automobiles for a long time. It seems to be a natural occurrence for humankind. Fast as a rabbit, loyal as a dog, young as a spring chicken. The list goes on and on. We connect with the animal kingdom more deeply than we may recognize. Allow the animal kingdom to speak to you. It may not speak our language, but it does speak volumes.

✚✚✚ EXERCISE 13 ✚✚✚
Team Building

What is your favorite animal? What is it that you like about this animal? It is likely that you identify in some way, shape, or form with these animals. This holds clues to various traits within your own personality. Get a group of friends together and ask everyone to talk about their favorite animal and their traits; others can comment to expand personal views. Discuss who each animal may get along with and which animals may not understand each other. This allows for personal development as well as group development and understanding. Am I suggesting a team-building exercise? Exactly!

The Plant Kingdom

Through connecting with the plant kingdom, we are able to recognize that different plants grow within different environments. So too will different people grow in different environments. Just because one person will thrive in a certain environment doesn't mean that we all must do so. Dialogue with plants. They show you how to grow, how to change, how to connect with those around you who are different than you are. They can also lead you to your purpose.

If you have a favorite plant, figure out what its purpose is and extract the basic wisdom for your life. Some of us are fruit trees; we produce nourishment for others. Some of us are flowers, and we simply make those around us happy. Some of us are corn, beans, and squash, as mentioned within chapter 3 of this book. What else does the plant kingdom show you? The tree tells me that I belong simply because I am here. The rosebush tells me that I can be beautiful in my own regard and that it is natural to have some thorny defense mechanisms. The plant kingdom is self-sustaining, which teaches me to think about sustainability.

Forest influences climate by affecting the amount of carbon dioxide within the earth's atmosphere through the process of photosynthesis. This carbon is stored in the leaves, bark, and roots. When a forest can collect more carbon than it releases, it is known as a carbon sink; they help to cool down the planet. However, when a forest is harvested, this carbon is released into the earth's atmosphere as carbon dioxide. This traps heat and warms the surface of the planet. I pray that the human race finds a way to honor the natural world. I pray that we take care of our eldest teacher. I pray.

Additionally, the plant kingdom and animal kingdom are two main components that create the landscapes we have here on Mother Earth. We are all connected! We are all one!

Landscapes

The landscape is the environment that the plants and animals live within. When we spoke about the animal kingdom, we began to identify personally with animals. The same phenomenon occurred when we looked at the plant kingdom; we personally identified with the plant. However, when we looked at the landscapes, things changed. We began to recognize the environments that we move in and out from. There is an internal world and there is an external environment. At times it is difficult to know whether we need to change the internal or external environments. Through journaling and/or speaking with trusted friends and family, the answer to this question will emerge.

Although we went through five different environments within this book, I would like to encourage you to investigate other environments as well. Maybe you live on the prairie; if so, walk out to the prairie and describe it with adjectives. These adjectives can then be applied to the environments and landscapes within relationships, careers, and health and well-being. Next, visit that same piece of land throughout the different seasons. Does it change? If so, how? This will give you more messages and wisdom from the natural world. You may also want to identify the types of animals that enjoy that landscape and apply that wisdom in your life. Notice what plants are in the landscape and apply that wisdom. Do this with any landscape, whether it is a meadow, a lake or pond, or maybe even the ocean. This is the natural world expressing to us that there are many different environments. It is not about the environment being good or bad; it is about the environment being a healthy place for you to grow, to thrive, and to be authentic.

At this point, I am hoping that you feel like speaking with your teacher, the natural world. Work with this wisdom as it brings deep insights into your world. They say that when the student is ready, the teacher will appear. Well, here she is—Mother Earth in all her wisdom!

The Seasons and Weather Cycles

The ancestors tell us that we roll through seasons much like Mother Earth rolls through seasons. However, our seasons are not necessarily three months long. Sometimes they can last for days and sometimes they can last for years. Spring, summer, autumn, and winter: each season has a theme with it. Spring is the time to plant. Summer is the time to grow. Autumn is the time to harvest. Winter is the time to go within.

However, there are other types of seasons that we move through in our life. The seasons of youth, adult, and elder. The season of cleansing, releasing, and clearing. The season of love, joy, and peace. The season of healing and rejuvenating. The season of change, be it little or big. Life, death, rebirth. There are many, many seasons within our lifetimes.

I had a season of being a waitress. Then I became a manager, followed by the season of corporate America. Next was the season of working for the government, and now is the season of self-employment. One season rolled into another season—one season ends and another begins. What is the season of your life? What were the themes within each of these seasons? All of this is your personal story and it is worth understanding and defining.

Each season has its own characteristics. Extract what they are for you. Remember, just because one season comes to an end doesn't mean that it is all over. The natural world invites us to lean into each season. If I don't know what season I am in, I would be unprepared for the season. Be who you are, be where you are, and be aware—this is what nature teaches us. May the seasons ahead of you hold beauty!

The Medicine Wheel

The medicine wheel may seem like a basic circle at first. But as we have delved into all of the aspects that can be contained within the medicine wheel, the wheel has become a dynamic teacher for recognizing all things and balancing these things within our lives. Whether you choose to work with a four-sectioned wheel or a larger wheel, make it your own.

There is an ancient Navajo teaching that reveals the purpose of life. It is said that the purpose in life is to continuously grow in our four bodies of existence—to seek balance as we grow. As simple as this may sound, growth and balance occur in countless ways. The medicine wheel is a model that allows us to do this.

Additionally, there is an old Navajo teaching about the sacred number four. Think about how many things can be categorized in fours: directions, seasons, bodies of existence, elements, etc. The story says the reason that so many basic concepts are sectioned into fours is because we are currently in the third dimension and the natural world is teaching us how to move into the next dimension—the fourth dimension. Pretty cool stuff, huh?

✚✚✚ EXERCISE 14 ✚✚✚
Medicine Wheel

You can do this on a piece of paper, create one in your home, or do this on the land. Whatever works best for you. The first step is to define the circle; draw it or create it with stones. Next, divide the circle into four equal parts. Working with the various categories in the previous section, list these in the circle. Continue by adding the animals that you align with to each of the four sections. Add a plant that makes sense to you in each section. Pick colors to make it your own. The art of creating your own circle will align your energy.

Finally, move into one of the four sections and see what is in there and how those things align with you and where you were at during that time in your life. Meditate on that and journal about what comes up within you. Continue to move through each section of the circle, meditating and journaling. Even if you haven't experienced your elder years yet, this will provide you with much insight. The whole process of creating your own circle, meditating on it, and journaling about each section will provide you with alignment, balance, and a deeper understanding of how life moves in circles. When one section has come to an end, it means that the next section can begin.

I personally choose to work with a four-pronged medicine wheel for the most part. However, when I look at the seasons of the year, I also implement an eight-pronged wheel to respect the changing of the equinox, the solstice, and the direct times in between: the Sabbats, which are sun celebrations.

Sabbats are holy days aligned with the seasonal calendar and the sun. The equinox (fall and spring), the solstice (winter and summer), and the times in between. There are a total of eight Sabbats to celebrate. In order:

- Samhain: The Celtic New Year. Around October 31. It is when the sun is fifteen degrees in Scorpio. Summer's end. Honor the dead.

- Yule: Winter solstice. Around December 21. It is when the sun is one degree in Capricorn. The moment when the wheel or the sun stands still. Honor the wheel as it stands still and will start to turn. The longest day of the moon and the returning of the sun.

- Imbolc: Around February 2. It is when the sun is fifteen degrees in Aquarius. First milk or in milk. Honoring the signs of new growth.

- Ostara: Spring equinox. Around March 21. It is when the sun is one degree in Aries. The mouth of beginnings or the mouth of opening. Return of the goddess from the underworld.

- Beltane: May Day. Around May 1. It is when the sun is fifteen degrees in Taurus. Bright fire or lucky fire. Honoring spring.

- Midsummer: Summer solstice. Around June 21. It is when the sun is one degree in Cancer. The longest day of the sun and the returning of the moon.

- Lammas: Around August 1. It is when the sun is fifteen degrees in Leo. Half mass. Honoring harvest and giving fruits back to the soil.

- Mabon: Fall equinox. Around September 21. It is when the sun is one degree in Libra. Divine youth. Honoring the second harvest and corn festival.

These are ancient traditions given to us by our elders. This is how they aligned with the seasons; this was their medicine wheel for planting and harvesting. I bring this up so that we can recognize that—although my ancestors wouldn't necessarily refer to this as a medicine wheel—it certainly is one to me. May we live in balance with nature and ourselves!

The Shadow Side

As I continuously befriend my shadow, I find that I have started to drop my defense mechanisms. I stopped taking things so personally. I believe that this will be a lifetime process for me, and I am willing to do this. However, one never knows; maybe I will accomplish this sooner than I expect!

As I drop my defense mechanisms, I find that I am in fewer altercations with others. There was a stint in my life when I took martial arts. One of the lessons that I gained from this experience is to step out of the way of a punch or hit. I still am a warrior, but I have set down my weapons and I have picked up skill. It is said that a young warrior needs to prove themselves so they look for war. However, an elder warrior has nothing left to prove—they have been there already, so elder warriors look for peace, not war. There was a time that I needed to prove myself to others, so I did everything I could to make them proud of me. One day I realized that I did not need to prove myself to them at all. I just needed to prove myself to myself.

My son is a leader. I saw this at a very early age, so I tried to nurture and guide that leader within him. One day when he was a teenager, he came home from school in a foul mood. I can't remember the exact situation, but I can remember what I told him. I told him that just because somebody takes a "dump" in front of you does not mean that you need to step in it. In life, people may do this intentionally or subconsciously. They may lay a load of crap before you and want you to engage. At this point, you have a choice. Knowing that you have a choice can at times make the biggest difference in the world, especially for a young man who is growing into a leader.

Leaders have a difficult path in this world. At times they need to take responsibility for their mistakes and give praise to those that they lead. Leaders benefit from understanding what it means to lead, not taking things too personally, and not having to engage in every battle. Only when one faces their own shadow can they completely and holistically lead others. We lead by example, don't we? Whether you are a leader in a large corporation, a small business, or your own life, I honor you and recognize you for all the sacrifices that you make. Be your greatness!

As you do the work to recognize, accept, and embrace your shadow, you will see other people's shadows more quickly. I have found that the more I accept my own shadow and embrace her, the less judgmental I am of others. However, it is good to remember that the people who do not face their own shadow will most likely project that shadow onto another. Be aware that this happens so you can recognize when it does.

Conclusion

If you have made it this far, thank you so much for taking this journey with me. Although this book was written with the hope that everyone reconnects with the natural world and sees the natural world as our eldest teacher, my underlying hope is to encourage, inspire, and empower you to be your authentic self—to give yourself permission to be you. You are the only energetic vibration on the face of this earth that can be you. You matter!

If there is a time when you don't feel like you belong, dialogue with a tree. If there is a time when you feel like you are not good enough, dialogue with an animal. If there is a time when you feel like you need permission to be who and what you are, dialogue with the seasons and the weather cycles. Whatever else comes your way within the natural world, dialogue with it. Being you is a birthright!

Everyone is authentic in my book. And therein lie our similarities. Sometimes in silence or during a meditative state, I imagine the end of my journey. What story do I want to tell? When I hear the story of my future self, I gain direction and know what to do today. Although there is great wisdom in the natural world, it is the still, small voice within your energetic vibration that understands what it is saying to you. You must be comfortable enough with the self to listen.

My hope is that you will continue to cultivate your own individual and authentic relationship with the natural world. I believe that it speaks with each of us in different ways and in different forms. I know that our ancestors were very connected to the natural world. When did we begin to separate from it? I am sure it didn't happen overnight. There must be many different belief systems and opinions out there to address this question. I would enjoy examining this question with you. Or maybe you should journal about it or discuss this topic with your friends. Maybe you already have your own understanding of it. I bring this up because whatever it was that wanted us to be disconnected from the natural world is most likely still around. We need to be able to recognize it and stand strong and tall together. At times, others will come to you with judgment for being your authentic self; please try not to take this too personally. I believe that these are the individuals who do not allow themselves to be authentic. Nature tells us that authenticity is natural.

In my personal opinion, and from my personal experience, I think there came a time in the history of the human race that some humans wanted to control the masses. In order to control the masses, they began to separate us. Separate us from each other with judgments. Separate us from ourselves with shame and guilt. And separate us from the natural world, or home. Whatever the reason, this book is to bring us together. To remind you that being authentic is a birthright—and to welcome us all home. I have experienced and seen in many societies and belief systems that people are denied a voice. We are denied our emotions, mind, and spirit. I believe that if you give yourself permission to listen to yourself, you gain and grow in consciousness. Know thyself and you will know the universe. Let's celebrate this life and the natural world.

I have one final tip that I wish to give you. As you continuously unfold your own authenticity, your presence will begin to inspire others to step into theirs. The more empowered you are to be who and what you are, the more empowerment you will give to another to do the same. It's not even in words that we do this; it is in our actions, and it is a sense that we carry with us. This allows others to be their authentic self around you. Spread the love! Go get 'em, tiger!

Bibliography

Abram, David. *The Spell of the Sensuous: Perception and Language in a More-Than-Human World.* New York: Vintage Books, 2012.

Alshami, Ali M. "Pain: Is It All in the Brain or the Heart?" *Current Pain and Headache Reports* 23 (2019). https://doi.org/10.1007/s11916-019-0827-4.

Andrews, Ted. *Animal Speak: The Spiritual & Magical Powers of Creatures Great and Small.* Woodbury, MN: Llewellyn Publications, 2010.

———. *Nature-Speak: Signs, Omens & Messages in Nature.* Jackson, TN: Dragonhawk Publishing, 2004.

Boggs, Joe. "Honeylocusts and Mastodons." Buckeye Yard & Garden Online. Ohio State University. January 2, 2018. https://bygl.osu.edu/node/959.

Bohm, David, and Robert A. Weinberg. *On Dialogue*. New York: Routledge, 1996.

Buhner, Stephen Harrod. *The Secret Teachings of Plants: The Intelligence of the Heart in the Direct Perception of Nature*. Rochester, NY: Bear & Company, 2004.

CommonLit Staff. "Freud's Theory of the Id, Ego, and Superego." *CommonLit*, 2015. https://www.commonlit.org/en/texts/freud-s-theory-of-the-id-ego-and-superego.

Fox, Nathan S., Jennifer S. Brennan, and Stephen T. Chasen. "Clinical Estimation of Fetal Weight and the Hawthorne Effect." *EJOG* 141 (2008) 111–14. https://doi.org/10.1016/j.ejogrb.2008.07.023.

Freud, Sigmund. "The Ego and the Id (1923)." *TACD Journal* 17, no. 1 (1989): 5–22. https://doi.org/10.1080/104671X.1989.12034344.

Gardner, Howard. *Frames of Mind: The Theory of Multiple Intelligences*. New York: Basic Books, 2011.

Herculano-Houzel, Suzana. "The Remarkable, Yet Not Extraordinary, Human Brain as a Scaled-Up Primate Brain and Its Associated Cost." *PNAS* 109 (2012): 10661–68. https://www.pnas.org/content/109/Supplement_1/10661.

Herrmann, Ned. "What Is the Function of the Various Brainwaves?" *Scientific American*, December 22, 1997. https://www.scientificamerican.com/article/what-is-the-function-of-t-1997-12-22/.

Isaacs, William. *Dialogue and the Art of Thinking Together: A Pioneering Approach to Communicating in Business and in Life*. New York: Currency, 1999.

Jung, C. G. *The Archetypes and the Collective Unconscious*. Vol. 9, bk. 1, of *The Collected Works of C. G. Jung*. Translated by R. F. C. Hull. Princeton, NJ: Princeton University Press, 1990.

———. *Mysterium Coniunctionis (Volume 14): An Inquiry into the Separation and Synthesis of Psychic Opposites in Alchemy*. Vol. 14 of *The Collected Works of C. G. Jung*. New York: Routledge, 2014.

Koechlin, Florianne. *Plant Whispers: A Journey through New Realms of Science*. Translated by Thomas Rippel. Basel, Switzerland: Lenos Verlag, 2015.

———. "Tomatoes Talk, Birch Trees Learn—Do Plants Have Dignity?" January 11, 2016. TED video, 14:36. https://www.youtube.com/watch?v=i8YnvMpcrVI&t=378s.

Koneya, Mele, and Alton Barbour. *Louder Than Words: Nonverbal Communication*. Columbus, OH: Merrill, 1976.

Kulkarni, Subhash, Julia Ganz, James Bayrer, Laren Becker, Milena Bogunovic, and Meenakshi Rao. "Advances in Enteric Neurobiology: The 'Brain' in the Gut in Health and Disease." *Journal of Neuroscience* 31 (2018): 9346–54. https://doi.org/10.1523/JNEUROSCI.1663-18.2018.

Lemann, Nicholas. "The IQ Meritocracy." *Time* 153, no. 12 (1999): 115–16.

Lopez, Barry. *Of Wolves and Men*. New York: Simon & Schuster, 1978.

McCullough, Joe. "Alpha State." *Joe-McCullough.com* (blog), January 19, 2013. http://joe-mccullough.com/alpha-state/.

Miller, George A. "The Test; Alfred Binet's Method of Identifying Subnormal Schoolchildren Sired the IQ Test." *Science '84* 5 (Nov. 1984): 55.

Nietzsche, Friedrich. *Beyond Good and Evil: Prelude to a Philosophy of the Future*. Translated by Walter Kaufmann. New York: Vintage Books, 1989.

—. *On the Genealogy of Morals*. Translated by Walter Kaufmann and R. J. Hollingdale. New York: Vintage Books, 1989.

Nunez, Christina. "Rainforests, Explained." *National Geographic*, May 15, 2019. https://www.nationalgeographic.com/environment/habitats/rain-forests/.

Rath, Tom, and Barry Conchie. *Strengths Based Leadership: Great Leaders, Teams, and Why People Follow*. New York: Gallup Press, 2008.

Reber, Arthur S. *The Penguin Dictionary of Psychology*. New York: Penguin Books, 1985.

Rinpoche, Yongey Mingyur, and Eric Swanson. *The Joy of Living: Unlocking the Secret and Science of Happiness*. New York: Harmony Books, 2007.

Speake, Jennifer, ed. *Oxford Dictionary of Proverbs*. 6th ed. Oxford: Oxford University Press, 2015.

Weizmann Institute of Science. "Quantum Theory Demonstrated: Observation Affects Reality." *ScienceDaily*, February 27, 1998. https://www.sciencedaily.com/releases/1998/02/980227055013.htm.

Whitcomb, Bill. *The Magician's Companion: A Practical and Encyclopedic Guide to Magical and Religious Symbolism*. St. Paul, MN: Llewellyn Publications, 1993.

Woodbury, Anthony C. *Counting Eskimo Words for Snow: A Citizen's Guide*. Austin, TX: University of Texas: 1991.

To Write to the Author

If you wish to contact the author or would like more information about this book, please write to the author in care of Llewellyn Worldwide Ltd. and we will forward your request. Both the author and publisher appreciate hearing from you and learning of your enjoyment of this book and how it has helped you. Llewellyn Worldwide Ltd. cannot guarantee that every letter written to the author can be answered, but all will be forwarded. Please write to:

Granddaughter Crow
⁒ Llewellyn Worldwide
2143 Wooddale Drive
Woodbury, MN 55125-2989

Please enclose a self-addressed stamped envelope for reply,
or $1.00 to cover costs. If outside the U.S.A., enclose
an international postal reply coupon.

Many of Llewellyn's authors have websites with additional information and resources. For more information, please visit our website at http://www.llewellyn.com.